MAR 15 2017

# RAW
# CAKE

Beautiful, nutritious and indulgent raw
desserts, treats, smoothies and elixirs

# RAW
# CAKE

Daisy Kristiansen
Leah Garwood-Gowers
of **THE HARDIHOOD**

St. Martin's Griffin
New York

This book is for informational purposes only. Neither the Author nor the Publisher is engaged in rendering medical advice. As each individual's experience may vary, readers, especially those who are pregnant or have existing health problems, should consult their physician or health care professional before changing their diet or taking supplements, Chinese medicines, or herbal remedies. Bee pollen can provoke a severe reaction if you have a pollen allergy. Avoid if pregnant or breastfeeding, or if you are taking blood-thinning medication. Individual readers are solely responsible for their own health care decisions, and neither the Author nor the Publisher accept responsibility for any adverse effects individuals may claim to experience, whether directly or indirectly, based on information contained herein. The fact that any individual, organization, or Web site is referred to in this work as a potential source of further information does not mean that the Author or the Publisher endorse that source or the specific information or recommendations they may provide.

www.stmartins.com

Library of Congress Cataloging-in-Publication Data Available Upon Request

ISBN 978-1-250-11756-4 (paper over board)
ISBN 978-1-250-11757-1 (e-book)

Our books may be purchased in bulk for promotional, educational, or business use. Please contact your local bookseller or the Macmillan Corporate and Premium Sales Department at (800) 221-7945, extension 5442, or by e-mail at MacmillanSpecialMarkets@macmillan.com.

First published 2017 by Bluebird an imprint of Pan Macmillan

First U.S. Edition: February 2017

10 9 8 7 6 5 4 3 2 1

# CONTENTS

# Introduction

This book is for those new to raw food, the experimental and those who are simply excited about getting more nourishment from their sweet treats.

Back in 2014, when we made our first raw chocolate brownies, we were absolute beginners – all we knew was that we wanted to make beautiful desserts using nothing but natural ingredients. The only rule we had was that raw cake by The Hardihood had to be abundant and flavorsome and never bland or boring. Through a lot of trial, error and spilt nut milk, we got to grips first with the basics and then with the complexities of raw dessert-making.

Since then, The Hardihood has become known for its crisp, minimal, luxurious aesthetic. Here we want to share with you how we created our products, our journey, and the tips and techniques that we've picked up along the way. Forget everything you thought you knew about making cakes without butter, eggs and flour – we're here to give raw a good name! Here we'll share our collection of recipes for raw cheesecake, chocolate indulgences, ice creams, pudding pots, breakfast bowls, smoothies, tonics and superfood blends.

Like a lot of things in life our most brilliant breakthroughs have been born from the ashes of disaster. We've had a lot of fun, though, and we try not to take cake-making too seriously. It's this lightheartedness that we want to pass on to you. Don't be afraid of failure. You're working with delicious, wholesome ingredients; however it looks in the end, we promise it'll taste great. Relax and enjoy it – everything tastes better when served with a smile.

## Our Story

We've been friends for nearly a decade, during most of which we lived together in an East London warehouse, back when rent was cheap. We met at a fancy dinner party that we'd both been persuaded to go to and it wasn't long before we realized that we were the only ones at the table giggling at each other's jokes. We took the long bus ride home to Hackney together and haven't stopped laughing since.

We didn't know, at first, that we were destined for a life of raw cake. Before dreaming up The Hardihood we worked in fashion and in lifestyle journalism. Like any self-respecting city dwellers, we were passionate about London's diverse food scene; we'd try somewhere new every week and delight in sharing our findings. Getting to know London through its best-loved dining spots we looked for innovative menus, fresh food and good vibes.

Soon we began to notice a rise in LA-inspired cold-press juice bars and Sydney-style cafés with a focus on wellness, and as our curiosity prompted us to travel around London for a taste of the good life, our intrigue grew with each feel-good food spot that we visited. The more far-out the dish, the more inspired we were; nut milk, matcha lattes, chia seeds, raw cacao – it was all new to us and we loved it. We discovered ayurveda, healing foods, holistic health and raw cuisine, sampled medicinal mushrooms, fermented vegetables and powdered roots and drank charcoal infusions. We felt like the world was onto something; people were beginning to

6

look at food in a different way, rejoicing in getting their five-a-day instead of being burdened by it. Accompanied by our New Year's resolution to give up refined sugar, this felt like an awakening. We became immersed in the idea of wellness and wondered why our local neighborhood didn't have more to offer. Growing tired of the trek across town, we decided to experiment with our own creations instead. We bought a food processor, a shed-load of dates, nuts and coconut oil, and got to work.

Looking back now, we laugh at our first attempts to master raw desserts – our trials mostly included chucking everything into a blender and hoping for the best. There were soggy cheesecakes, droopy brownies and crumbly flapjacks, but miraculously, we weren't deterred. We loved this new approach to baking and were as excited about the journey as we were about the destination.

In the early days we formulated creations from our kitchens at home, as although we no longer lived together our houses were a five-minute walk away. We'd spend all of our spare time trying out new recipes, sourcing ingredients and reading up on techniques. We bought the books and became friendly with our local greengrocers so that they'd let us purchase in bulk. We tested everything we made on our male friends as well as female, because we knew that when it came to cake they wouldn't really care that something was good for them, we knew they'd just give it to us straight. We were adamant that our cakes would always be absurdly delicious, not just a "free-from" alternative.

Because our creations are so visual we documented the whole thing on Instagram from the start; we learned how to style the cakes and became enthralled with kitchenware, ceramics, tea towels – you name it. We built up a repertoire of recipes that we were proud of and began to receive orders, first from our friends, then from people who'd heard about us through word of mouth or online. As the weeks went by we'd make an increasing number of cakes, getting more adventurous with each order.

In the winter of 2015 we were invited to sell cakes at Paris Fashion Week. We were delighted and agreed immediately, thinking we'd figure out the logistics later. In the end we took the Eurostar with seven suitcases and the help of Daisy's husband. We had our ingredients delivered to a depot on the outskirts of Paris and used Airbnb to transform someone's kitchen into a production unit. It was probably one of our most brilliantly ridiculous adventures to date, topped only by returning the following year by car and doing the same thing all over again. Introducing the international fashion crowd to raw cake was transformational and we've worked hand in hand with the fashion industry ever since.

We outgrew our home kitchens pretty quickly and soon began looking for something more functional. Our only prerequisites were that the space would have good natural light and plenty of room for fridges, but aside from that we were happy to have any space that we could call our own. As it happens, we got lucky, really lucky, and we moved into a studio in the center of the area we had set out to transform. We have a skylight, exposed beams and a garden, and we definitely know how good we've got it.

Signing the lease on our own studio kitchen was pivotal. We were able to dedicate all of our time to our passion, filling the cupboards with all sorts of superfoods, herbs and tinctures. We hired our first employee and became a tiny team of three, learning a little bit more each day about creating beautiful desserts using natural, raw ingredients.

7

## Why Raw?

It was through our commitment to find a way to make delicious desserts that were free from refined sugar and processed ingredients that we discovered raw cuisine, a plant-based style of preparing food in which components aren't heated above a certain temperature. The exact temperature is disputed, with some saying 105°F and others saying 120°F. We settle for around 110°F.

We love raw desserts because the ingredients we use are naturally free from refined sugar, gluten, dairy and soy, and are worlds away from processed 'free-from' foods, which are often loaded with substitutes to replace whichever food group they're trying to avoid (and aren't necessarily healthier). We love pushing the limits of raw, natural, superfood ingredients to create the best possible confectionery, in every way. And there's no denying that we feel great eating this way.

First, though, we want to be clear. Neither of us eats an entirely raw diet. London is often chilly and we wake up craving a hot bowl of porridge or soup. Really, it's about listening to your body and doing what feels best for it based on the information that you have. The cravings we used to have for pick 'n' mix candies and Ben & Jerry's now feel more like cravings for raw Snickers bars or our Salted Caramel Crunch Bars. As our consciousness around food shifted, so did our cravings. It's all part of a learning process and a journey that is to be enjoyed.

## The Hardihood Philosophy

The Hardihood philosophy is simple; we believe that people should have complete freedom of choice when it comes to what they're putting into their bodies and shouldn't have to compromise on flavor or decadence in doing so. We're foodies at heart, and because of this our Raw Cake creations will always be every bit as delicious as the desserts you grew up with, only with the added benefit of nutritious ingredients. This lifestyle is most definitely not about going without; it's about embracing what makes your body feel good, what makes you happy and the numerous ways you can have your cake and eat it.

Sharing our journey with you feels like a natural getting together with friends. We don't want to keep our discoveries to ourselves, we want to get out there and share the good vibes! We live in a world where it's easier to meaningfully connect to the internet than each other – now more than ever we need to make a conscious effort to treat people right in real time and eat real food while we're at it.

## Modern Alchemy

Like most people, we grew up trying to believe in magic: *The Craft*, *Hocus Pocus*, *The Worst Witch*, *Charmed*... Of course, the rational brain knew it all along, but there was still a part of us that cried when we realized we would never receive a letter of acceptance from Hogwarts. The next few years were spent mainly forgetting about enchantment and learning how to become grown-ups. Believing in Flower Fairies and casting spells over garden-foraged potions of pinecones, pebbles and vacant snail shells faded like distant memories. It wasn't until later that we rediscovered alchemy – in the form of healing herbs, elixirs and tonics. We've learned to balance our bodies' needs by supplementing our diets with herbs and superfoods that add flavor, color, depth and healing to our meals. It's fascinating.

By using natural ingredients and ancient wisdom, we support the chemistry of the human body while having fun and creating beautiful food. These days it's easy to grab a bag of spirulina or maca from your local supermarket, and for the more unusual ingredients we usually head to a health food shop or the internet. Trust us, though, the hunt for the obscure is all part of the enjoyment; we were like kids in a candy shop when we got to run wild in LA for a week, buying up all of the powders, pills and pastilles we'd heard of and those we'd not heard of!

## Getting Started

If this is your first foray into the world of raw, don't be nervous – we were you not so long ago. One of the great things about raw baking is its simplicity. Unlike traditional baking, it's not an exact science, so it leaves plenty of room for creativity and constructive failure. We find working with wholesome natural ingredients rewarding because they're so pure. You know exactly what you're going to get out of a recipe because you know exactly what you put into it. Working with foods that only have the name of one ingredient listed on the back of the packaging is liberating.

## Feel Free to Experiment

There are many ways to expand on the recipes in this book and there are many ways to simplify them. When we first began reading raw recipe books we were bewildered by how complicated they were and the length of the ingredient lists. We began to excel at improvisation and we urge you to improvise, too. If you're about to start preparing your dessert and suddenly realize you don't have enough of something in stock, experiment by replacing it with something similar. The same can be said for superfood powders – if you don't have a specific ingredient

in your cupboard already or you're waiting for it to arrive after ordering it online (this happens to us all the time), don't be afraid to use something else. There are no rules here and, who knows, you might find a variation that works better for you this way.

You can simplify this even more by making your own ingredients if you have the time. There's something very satisfying about seeing the ingredients in one form one minute and then minutes later they're setting in the fridge, unaltered, only presented differently.

## Back to the Future

Eating as organically as possible allows us to return to our roots and to how our great grandparents ate. It is also a great way to connect to nature if you are living in a busy city. Of course, eating home-grown or organic produce is not only good for our bodies but also for the environment. Minimizing pesticides, synthetic fertilizers, hormones and antibiotics means that the produce is fresher and less toxic. Organic farming methods reduce soil and water contamination, help preserve local wildlife, encourage biodiversity and are generally more sustainable.

## Inspiration and Influence

Travel is the source of inspiration that we tap into repeatedly when we are coming up with ideas for The Hardihood. It was upon returning from respective trips to Japan and Ibiza that The Hardihood was initially founded, and we revisit our mental scrapbooks regularly.

### Ibiza

Leah has family in Ibiza and over the years has spent many joyful summers frolicking in the rural beauty of the island. Rising with the

sun became a tradition for us in Ibiza and when we explored the island together we'd drive down dust-covered tracks to a different cove each morning, capturing the light on camera before dipping into the ocean and swimming in whichever direction the tide took us. Once we'd had enough we'd clamber onto the rocks and soak up the morning rays, only half watching as the sun turned our soggy footprints to ghosts.

To a backdrop of Bohemian campsites, jagged cliff edges and dramatic coastlines, Leah grew up experiencing the serenity of the wilderness, its vastness disrupted only by wildlife and the sound of the wind. It's this connection to nature that we focus on when we need to cultivate a little space in our excitable city lives; a peaceful sensation to call upon when life picks up pace.

## Copenhagen

For Daisy, marrying a Dane has meant making Copenhagen her second home. Like the calm water that runs through the city to the wild, windswept beaches, there's a settled sense of serenity in this sleepy toy-town. Breathing in the crisp air as you plod along the winding canals you realize that there's no reason to move any faster. Here, nothing is rushed; architecture, design, life, it's all carried out with the same considered precision. Scandinavian minimalism is no accident.

Scavenger bike rides to the summerhouse allotment to forage for wild rose hips, fresh blueberries, gooseberries, blackberries, lemon balm and stevia interweave the city with nature seamlessly. Evening meals are put together using the day's finds and are relished with friends and family. The Danish word *Hygge* describes this heart-warming energy, and although there isn't a direct translation we see it simply as the Danish ritual of enjoying life's simple pleasures. Time spent with loved ones is savored, and creating a beautiful environment in which to share moments is an important part of this.

## Japan

A visual roller coaster of bright lights and colors you've never seen before, there's nowhere in the world that pushes you as deliciously close to sensory overload as Japan. A rocket ride into the world of the unknown, every moment is experienced in high definition. If our minds had memory cards they'd have been full in a heartbeat. Every unknown food has to be tasted, every texture touched, every graphic storefront admired and every oddity recorded. Mouth open in awe is how we took in Tokyo.

It was Daisy's 2014 trip here that ignited a feverous passion for packaging, a penchant for the well-presented. Without understanding a word of the language, Japanese branding speaks loud and clear. No opportunity to exhibit excellence is wasted; even tea leaves are wrapped to perfection. In the largest city in the world, where it feels like somebody hit fast forward, time stands still when it comes to tradition.

## Los Angeles

We touched down on California turf after 11 hours of excited squirming on a tightly packed British Airways flight. We'd booked the trip to our dream destination on a whim and given ourselves a week in which to satisfy our expectations. The balmy coastal warmth welcomed us from the airport, the sky was clear and we winked at the moon and the stars in the magic of the moment.

When we woke the next morning our neighborhood was full of single-story buildings and the views were stretching way out into the horizon. Palm trees towered over Silver Lake as the sun rose over the city. We were surrounded by space and our eyes reveled in remembering how to use the full range of their vision as we looked into the distance. Urban cacti and succulents grew freely in the streets and punctuated our stroll to a yoga class that morning. The mismatched houses and villas existed without correlation, an endless spectrum of colors and shades. The light broke through the branches of botanical plants, casting our giddy shadows in the California light.

We ventured to our local Moon Juice where we met Jeremy, our dear friend and seasoned LA tour guide, before driving top-down in his Mustang to visit a food show in Anaheim as palm tree silhouettes dusted the sky. Even before we visited the Rose Bowl Flea Market, House of Intuition and Café Gratitude, we knew that we were madly, truly, deeply in love with the wild, wild West Coast.

## *London*

London is home; it's the city in which we dreamt up The Hardihood over two cups of tea on a cold evening in January. It's under this skyline that we went on mad hunts for mesquite; ran a tab with our local organic shop to fund our first recipe trials; discovered raw chocolate and the uplifting benefits of cacao, a million miles from the ancient civilizations of South America. The city we live in has become our inspiration, our teacher and our motivation.

From the age-old establishments that have been going against the grain since day dot, committed to keeping it organic before people were prepared to pay more for it, to the innovative start-ups that have risked it all to bring a new perspective to the market as well as those who are simply courageous enough to try something new; you're the reason why we love this city, we know you'll always keep us on our toes, reaching for the stars.

## Energy: An Afterword

The Hardihood began life as a labor of love and we feel grateful every day that it's developed into something that's able to sustain us. We've learned to believe in our creative ability, and we now know that listening to our hearts will seldom take us down the wrong path in the long run. We try to release attachments to outcomes and let progress show up in whatever way it likes, so we can celebrate every breakthrough, no matter what it is.

Investing in our hopes, dreams and longings is as important as investing in our bodies. Take time for yourself, show your friends how much they mean to you and smile at strangers in the street; kindness costs nothing and we try to sprinkle it on everything. We do our best to stay away from envy, jealousy and bad vibes and surround ourselves with the people who inspire us. We have also learned how to say no.

Believe in magic, believe in healing and believe in building the most brilliant life that you could ever imagine for yourself. Stay in your power and trust your gut. Never show up empty handed to a party or closed minded to a conversation, allow yourself to embrace your quiet side and to dance with your inner party animal. You are unique; find your magic and commit to staying there.

13

# Equipment

If you want to keep it raw, when it comes to equipment there are a few bits that are essential to kick-start your journey.

If you're only just starting out and you don't have much equipment yet, begin with cheaper models of some gear and then upgrade to something more powerful – and expensive! – as you get The Hardihood Raw Cake bug.

## Food Processor

You won't get very far without a food processor, but this doesn't mean that you need to splash out on a really expensive model. Start small like we did and who knows, you might end up with a whole family of whizzing, blending, shredding machines one day.

Essential for fine-chopping nuts, dates and seeds, a food processor breaks down anything you put in it and, unlike a blender, it won't conk out without liquid. Again the more high-powered the better, but we got great results from our trusty $70 entry level model for at least the first two years of experimenting, and we're actually far too attached to it so it still sits alongside the super-powerful industrial machines we use now.

## Blender

There are many different blenders on the market and our advice is to pretty much avoid the cheaper models and wait until you can afford something more mid-range. You'll need something quite high speed for getting creams and liquids really smooth. If you can't swing a good model now, you can use a food processor instead, but the results won't be quite as smooth.

## Dehydrator

Dehydrators vary vastly in quality and in price. In all honesty you don't desperately need one – we didn't have one for a long time, and none of the recipes in this book require one – but if you're lucky enough to have space in your kitchen for one or happen to have one already, consider it a blessing. They're a bit of an eyesore but are great for drying out raw dough or decorative fruit without using too much warmth. If you don't have a dehydrator, you can use your oven, set to 110°F, leaving the items to dry for a long period of time. However, dehydrators are much more economically and environmentally friendly than leaving your oven on.

14

# Pre–cake Prep

## Soaking Nuts

Not only are soaked nuts smoother and creamier when blended but they're prepared in a way that grants our bodies access to the full range of nutritional benefits without the worry of gut irritation. Prepping them basically just involves soaking overnight to remove the phytates and enzyme inhibitors that surround them to protect them from predators or sprouting too early. If a recipe calls for soaked nuts, measure out the quantity that you need and then add them to a jar or bowl and cover them with cool filtered water and leave overnight. If you need to speed up the process, use warm water and cover for a few hours, checking periodically to see if they're ready. You're looking for a spongy absorbent consistency. Be sure to drain the water and give the nuts a rinse before either letting them dry in the dehydrator or oven or using them while wet.

## Soaking Dates

We often find that no two bags of dates are the same: some are soft and gooey while others are rock solid. To soften dates and make them stickier, we soak them in two ways: either in cold filtered water overnight or in warm water for an hour or less. Sometimes, if you're using them in a smoothie or a sauce, you'll want a soft and runny consistency like a syrup, but at other times, if they are to be used as a binding agent in a base, the recipe will call for a firmer, tacky consistency. Use your judgment as to whether dates are soft enough; it'll depend on a few factors: how powerful your blender is, the desired consistency of the mixture, and which dates you're using. Medjool dates rarely need soaking for long, unless you're looking to achieve a syrupy or liquid consistency.

## Melting Coconut Oil

Coconut oil is hugely versatile. It can be used solid at room temperature or cooler, and as a liquid when heated. We use a lot of liquid coconut oil because pouring it into cups minimizes wastage and it is much easier and faster to work with. In order to melt the coconut oil, we pour lukewarm water into a container and place the jar of coconut oil in it with the lid on, ensuring that none of the water gets into the oil. Once it has turned to liquid we use it straight away or within the next half hour to make sure it doesn't reset.

Making Your Own Ingredients

**Chapter 1**

**Making your own ingredients** is a great place to start if you've just begun your journey into raw. These simple recipes are not only the building blocks for a lot of the desserts that we make, but also for our day-to-day lives. Although it's easier to find really good-quality nut butters and nut milks in the shops these days, we always keep a few jars of homemade nut milk in the fridge and nut butters on the shelf, and our friends have even been known to receive them as gifts on special occasions. One of the keys to making your own is never throwing away your empty jars – wash them thoroughly and put them away; that way you'll always have something to store your creations in.

# Nut & Seed Butters

Nuts and seeds can be a fantastic source of energy, some B vitamins, vitamin E, zinc, iron, manganese, potassium, magnesium, calcium, fiber and protein, and they have the added bonus of containing antioxidants and essential fatty acids. Flax seeds, hemp seeds and walnuts are the best options if you're looking for omega-3 fats. Nuts and seeds are the perfect snack to help lower cholesterol, though do be aware they are pretty high in calories because of all those healthy fats.

However, although nuts and seeds are considered to be a healthy option, we cannot absorb their beneficial nutrients fully without first soaking them. This is because raw nuts contain enzyme inhibitors and phytates that naturally protect them until proper growing conditions occur, ensuring that the nut or seed will not sprout prematurely.

Soaking them is a simple process. Place the nuts in a medium-large bowl or jar and cover with cold filtered water. Leave the bowl in a cool, shaded place covered with a clean tea towel (see soaking times in the box on the left), and then once the required time is up, drain the nuts, discard the water, rinse the nuts in fresh running water and drain again.

Set aside the nuts to dry off, then dehydrate them in a dehydrator – if you have one – or alternatively, use your oven, set no higher than 110°F or at its nearest low temperature. Spread the nuts out evenly on a baking tray and place in the oven for 12–16 hours, turning the nuts occasionally to make sure they are drying evenly.

## Soaking Times

There are differing views as to how long each type of nut or seed needs to be soaked, depending on the particular variety and as a result of their different levels of absorbency and minerals, but this is what works for us:

| | |
|---|---|
| Almonds | 8–10 hours |
| Brazil nuts | None |
| Cashews | 2 hours |
| Flax seeds | 8 hours |
| Hazelnuts | 8 hours |
| Hemp seeds | None |
| Macadamias | 8 hours |
| Peanuts | 8–10 hours |
| Pecans | 6 hours |
| Pine nuts | 8 hours |
| Pistachios | None |
| Pumpkin seeds | 6 hours |
| Sesame seeds | 6–8 hours |
| Sunflower seeds | 2 hours |
| Walnuts | 6 hours |

# How to Make Nut & Seed Butters

## Maca almond butter
2 cups almonds, soaked for
   8-10 hours, rinsed, drained
   and dehydrated
1 tablespoon maca powder
2 tablespoons coconut sugar
2 tablespoons melted coconut oil
pinch of Himalayan salt

## Baobab peanut butter
2 cups peanuts, soaked for
   8-10 hours, rinsed, drained
   and dehydrated
1 tablespoon baobab powder
2 tablespoons coconut sugar
2 tablespoons melted coconut oil
pinch of Himalayan salt

## Cashew cinnamon butter
2 cups cashews, soaked for
   2 hours, rinsed, drained and
   dehydrated
2 teaspoons ground cinnamon
2 tablespoons coconut sugar
3 tablespoons melted coconut oil
pinch of Himalayan salt

First, decide on any flavorings you might want to include, such as dates, vanilla powder, ground cinnamon, grated nutmeg, coconut sugar, maple syrup, ground ginger, turmeric, cacao, maca, lucuma or chaga powders or coconut nectar, etc. Choose your favorites and be creative! We've listed the ingredients for our top three favorite nut butters on the left.

Once you've decided on your nuts or seeds and flavors, place the quantity of your chosen nuts in your food processor (see *TIP*) and blend on high until they break down to a powder, then stop and scrape down the sides as many times as necessary to work the mixture back in. Keep processing for a further 10 minutes, then pour in the melted coconut oil. If you don't love the taste of coconut oil, try a "cuisine" oil – a flavorless version.

Continue blending for a further 5–10 minutes until the butter becomes smooth and creamy. This can take a while longer depending on your machine, but keep on going even if you think it's not working!

Sprinkle in a pinch of high-quality salt at the end, as this brings out the sweet flavors of the nuts or seeds and gives the butter a richer, more balanced taste.

*TIP:* Using a high-powered processor will help a lot when making nut butters, as you need a strong motor that will not conk out over the longer blending times! We use a Magimix, Robot Coupe – all of which are fantastic.

# Nut Milks

Nut milks are an invaluable addition to any fridge – they're a dairy-free alternative with benefits. We drink them in the morning for a nutrient-rich, plant-based protein boost or in the evening blended with ginger and ashwagandha for a soothing bedtime tipple. We also use them in cakes, puddings and smoothies.

Just as for nut butters (see pages 19–20), soaking nuts before blending them to use in milks is important, not just for preserving their nutritional benefits and making them easier to digest, but also because it helps with the blending stage itself – fully soaked nuts blend more smoothly and leave less pulp behind.

# How to Make Nut Milks

Place the nuts in a medium-large bowl and cover with cold filtered water, adding a pinch of Himalayan salt. Leave the bowl in a cool, shaded place, covered with a clean tea towel (see soaking times on page 19), then once the required time is up, drain the nuts, discard the water, rinse the nuts under fresh running water and drain again.

Blend with fresh filtered water in a high-powered blender on high at a ratio of 4 parts water to 1 part nuts. At this stage, add in any extra flavorings that you'd like.

For a smooth texture, pour the blended liquid through a nut milk bag (available at many natural food stores) into a large bowl or jug; discard the pulp left in the bag.

If you want to save money on ingredients and curb the high price tag of homemade nut milks, replace half the nuts with soaked brown rice.

# Strawberry
# & Almond Milk

1½ cups almonds, soaked for
   8-10 hours
1 quart (4 cups) filtered water
2 cups strawberries
2 tablespoons açai powder
1 tablespoon coconut syrup or
   other liquid natural sweetener
½ teaspoon vanilla powder
pinch of Himalayan salt

Drain the almonds and rinse in fresh water. Blend on high in a high-powered blender with the water. Add the strawberries, açai powder, coconut syrup, vanilla and salt and pulse again for 1–2 minutes.

Pour through a nut milk bag into a large bowl or measuring cup, discard the pulp left in the bag, and store the nut milk in a clean, sealed bottle in the fridge for 2–3 days.

# Cashew
# & Maca Milk

22

1 cup cashews, soaked for
   2 hours, rinsed and draine
1 quart (4 cups) filtered water
3 Medjool dates, pitted
½ teaspoon vanilla powder
1 tablespoon maca powder
pinch of Himalayan salt

Drain the cashews and rinse in fresh water. Blend on high in a high-powered blender with the water. Add the dates, vanilla, maca and salt and pulse again for 1–2 minutes.

Pour through a nut milk bag into a large bowl or measuring cup, discard the pulp left in the bag, and store the nut milk in a clean, sealed bottle in the fridge for 2–3 days.

*Above*: Strawberry & Almond Milk

making your own ingredients

# Date & Hemp Seed Milk

SERVES 4–6

1 cup shelled hemp seeds
1 quart (4 cups) filtered water
5 Medjool dates, pitted
pinch of Himalayan salt

Hemp seeds do not need soaking, so this is a quick and easy recipe with no prep time. Blend all the ingredients in a high-powered blender on high for 1–2 minutes until smooth.

Pour through a nut milk bag into a large bowl or measuring cup, discard the pulp left in the bag, and store the seed milk in a clean, sealed bottle in the fridge for 2–3 days.

# Pistachio & Cinnamon Milk

SERVES 4–6

1 cup shelled pistachios
1 quart (4 cups) filtered water
2 tablespoons coconut syrup
   or other liquid natural
   sweetener
½ tablespoon ground cinnamon
pinch of Himalayan salt

Pistachios do not require soaking before using, so just blend all the ingredients in a high-powered blender on high for 1–2 minutes until smooth.

Pour through a nut milk bag into a large bowl or measuring cup, discard the pulp left in the bag, and store the nut milk in a clean, sealed bottle in the fridge for up to 3 days.

# Hazelnut & Cacao Milk

SERVES 4–6

1 cup hazelnuts, soaked for
   8 hours
1 quart (4 cups) filtered water
2 tablespoons cacao powder
2 tablespoons maple syrup or
   coconut syrup
½ teaspoon vanilla powder
pinch of Himalayan salt

Drain the hazelnuts and rinse in fresh water. Blend in a high-powered blender with all the other ingredients on high for 1–2 minutes until smooth.

Pour through a nut milk bag into a large bowl or measuring cup, discard the pulp left in the bag, and store the nut milk in a clean, sealed bottle in the fridge for up to 3 days.

*Above*: Pistachio & Cinnamon Milk

making your own ingredients

# Date
# Paste

Date paste is tricky to get hold of. We've stumbled upon it for sale once from a renowned Turkish restaurateur; it was delicious, but it's just as easy to make your own.

Date paste is one of those things you can't believe is made from just one ingredient. It looks, tastes and behaves just like the caramel that we know and love – only it's better for you.

The best dates to use are the soft Medjool dates, as this large variety has a sumptuous, caramel-like flavor. If you can't get your hands on those, soaking other types of date until they are softer will work just as well.

2 cups pitted dates
1–2 tablespoons water or
    coconut oil (optional)
pinch of Himalayan salt

**MAKES ABOUT 2 CUPS**

Blend the dates in a high-powered food processor on high, stopping to scrape the sides down a few times, then blend for a couple more minutes until a paste starts to form. If you are finding that the dates are not blending to a smooth paste, add 1–2 tablespoons of water or coconut oil to help them along. Add the salt for a well-rounded, rich, sweet flavor and pulse briefly to combine.

# Raw
# Chocolate

When you don't have the time to temper your chocolate or be a fully fledged chocolatier, this is a simplified raw chocolate recipe that is really easy to whip up in a minute or two. It's not stable enough to be an ingredient for chocolate bars, but it's perfect for decorating your desserts with, pouring over ice cream or smothering your raw pancakes in. What's not to love?

¾ cup melted coconut oil
½ cup rice malt syrup or
    coconut syrup
¾ cup cacao powder

**MAKES ABOUT 2 CUPS**

Blend all the ingredients together in a high-powered food processor on high for a few seconds until well combined – taking care not to overmix. Et voilà!

*Above*: Raw Chocolate

making your own ingredients

Raw Breakfasts

Chapter 2

**A fresh hit of nutrients first thing** in the morning is a great way to start the day, best foot forward. Sometimes we're up and at it in five minutes flat and sometimes we're easy like Sunday morning, but either way we like to enjoy our breakfast. Juices and tonics are great if you wake up feeling like you need some refreshment after a late night; we often stumble into the kitchen and whiz up one of these with our eyes still half closed. Show yourself, your family, your housemate or your guests that you care by whipping up something as the sun comes up.

# Chocolate Clean Shake

Think the thick, gloopy chocolate milkshakes of your youth infused with the feel-good benefits of your future. Drinking this in the morning is like turning up the volume of your finest self. We skip down the street after dosing up on this. (*Pictured on pages 28-29.*)

1 banana

1 cup almond or other nut milk

2 tablespoons cacao powder

3 Medjool dates, pitted

1 tablespoon reishi powder (optional)

1 tablespoon coconut sugar (optional)

sprinkle of ground cinnamon

pinch of Himalayan salt

SERVES 1—2

Place all the ingredients except the coconut sugar in a high-powered blender and blend on high until completely smooth. Taste, and if you would like it a little sweeter, add the coconut sugar or another natural sweetener of your choice.

# Nutty Cacao Spread

We don't want to say that this is like Nutella, because it's so much better! A perfect raw treat that can be enjoyed spread on toast, rye bread, pancakes or bananas, or simply eaten with a spoon straight from the jar.

1 cup hazelnuts, soaked for 6–8 hours

½ cup pecans, soaked for 6–8 hours

½ cup cashews, soaked for 6–8 hours

¾ cup coconut syrup

½ cup cacao powder

⅓ cup melted coconut oil

½ teaspoon vanilla powder

2-3 tablespoons lukewarm water

¼ teaspoon Himalayan salt

SERVES 2

Drain and rinse the soaked nuts under cold running water, drain again, then place in a high-powered food processor and blend on high for 7–8 minutes. Add the rest of the ingredients and keep processing, scraping down the sides occasionally. The mixture will stay coarse and grainy for some time, and you may find that it takes 15–20 minutes, depending on the power of your machine. For an ultra-silky smooth texture, we finish off the spread in a blender for a few minutes.

Keep in a sealed jar in the fridge for up to 5 days.

# Breakfast Thyme Strawberry Smoothie

Complementing sweet flavors with savory herbs is something we love to do; the thyme in this smoothie absolutely sets it apart from the rest. It's a wholesome, well-rounded favorite that we love to kick off the weekend with. We like to dress it with the edible flowers that we grow in the garden, but if you're in a hurry this is a great one to pour into a jar and eat on the go.

1 banana, frozen
1 small cucumber or half
    a medium cucumber
7–8 strawberries
half a lemon, peeled
1 tablespoon flax seeds
2 tablespoons almonds
1 tablespoon pumpkin seeds
1 tablespoon peanut butter
½-inch piece of fresh ginger
    root, peeled
4 small thyme sprigs, plus more
    for an optional garnish
¼–½ cup almond milk
    (depending on how runny
    you want your smoothie)
squeeze of lime juice
edible flowers, for a garnish
    (optional)

**SERVES 1–2**

Place all the ingredients except the flowers in a high-powered blender and blend on high until smooth, using as much almond milk as you like to get the smoothie to your preferred consistency.

Serve straight away, garnished with a few thyme sprigs and flowers if you like.

> ### Thyme
> An herb from the mint family, aromatic thyme makes a great addition to smoothies and drinks, and pairs perfectly with fruits, nuts and seeds. It's hardy too, so easy to grow at home: pop a pot on your windowsill and watch it thrive.

raw breakfasts

# Creamy Green Smoothie

This does exactly what it promises: With all of the creamiest smoothie ingredients plus the prebiotic qualities of baobab and the optional immunity-boosting qualities of cordyceps (see page 183), this drink will wow everyone who tastes it.

1½ bananas
flesh of 1 small avocado
1 lime, peeled
2 tablespoons cashews
1 tablespoon baobab powder
1 tablespoon cordyceps
    powder (optional)
large splash of almond milk,
    plus more as you wish

SERVES 1—2

Place all the ingredients in a high-powered blender and blend on high until smooth, using as much almond milk as you like to get the smoothie to your preferred consistency.

# Mint Green Smoothie

This was inspired by a smoothie we tried in LA. The cacao nibs give it that extra crunch and the arugula takes it up a notch in terms of spice. We like to include arugula in our smoothies and juices because it contains DIM (Dindolylmethane), a great natural hormone balancer and fat breakdown stimulator.

2 bananas
handful of spinach
handful of arugula
2 Medjool dates, pitted
6 mint sprigs (stalks as well
    as leaves)
2 tablespoons shelled hemp
    seeds
2 tablespoons pumpkin seeds
1 tablespoon cacao nibs
¼ teaspoon vanilla powder
splash of almond milk

SERVES 1—2

Place all the ingredients in a high-powered blender and blend on high until smooth and creamy.

raw breakfasts

# Spirulina & Apricot Breakfast Bars

Good mornings start with one of these nutritionally packed bars in one hand and a warm drink in the other. These easy bars are filled with goodness and will set you off on your day in fighting form. Keep a batch in the fridge for the week or devour in one swoop.

1 cup dried apricots

1 cup gluten-free rolled oats

2 tablespoons chia seed

¼ cup golden flax seeds

2 tablespoons shelled hemp seeds

½ cup pumpkin seeds

½ cup goji berries

¼ cup date syrup or maple syrup

⅓ cup almond butter

1½ tablespoons spirulina powder

pinch of Himalayan salt

**MAKES 6—8 BARS**

---

Line a shallow 6- or 8-inch square baking pan with parchment paper.

Place the apricots in a high-powered food processor and pulse until coarsely chopped. Add the oats, flax seeds, hemp seeds, pumpkin seeds and goji berries and pulse again a few more times to combine everything.

Transfer the apricot mixture to a bowl and add the date syrup, almond butter and spirulina powder, then add the salt. Mix together by hand, making sure the apricot mixture is evenly coated with the almond butter and syrup.

Press the mixture into the baking pan (form a 6-inch square if using an 8-inch pan) and refrigerate for 3–4 hours or overnight before cutting into 6–8 chunky bars. Store in the fridge for up to 1 week.

*Spirulina*
A brilliant source of plant protein, several B vitamins and iron, spirulina boosts this breakfast bar's credentials no end. Buy organic spirulina if you can get hold of it.

raw breakfasts

raw cake

# Apple & Ginger Chia Seed Pudding

Chia seeds are such a versatile blessing. As they're known for their energy-giving abilities, it makes sense to begin the day with them. The addition of ginger to this scrumptious pudding gives it an extra kick and will assist in the smooth digestion of meals.

1 apple, cored, plus more,
　thinly sliced, for serving
½-inch piece of fresh ginger
　root, peeled and chopped
¾ cup nut milk
1 tablespoon maple syrup
¼ cup chia seeds
coconut yogurt, for serving

SERVES 1

---

Blend the apple with the ginger, nut milk and maple syrup in a high-powered blender on high until completely smooth.

Pour into a bowl and add the chia seeds, mixing them in with a spoon until well combined, then place in the fridge for 30 minutes–1 hour until the chia seeds have expanded and the mixture is gel-like. Add a dollop of coconut yogurt, dot with a few apple slices and serve immediately.

# Red Root Savory Smoothie

When we've eaten cake all day, there are times when we just crave something light and savory. Love at first sip, this is a great source of antioxidants and anti-inflammatory ingredients. Breakfast, lunch or dinner, this fragrant blend is reminiscent of a creamy take on gazpacho.

half a medium beet

4 medium slicing tomatoes or
    8 small plum tomatoes

half a medium carrot

1 cup filtered water

¼ cup macadamia nuts

¼ cup almond milk

half a medium-size hot chili
    pepper (with its seeds)

½-inch piece of fresh ginger
    root, peeled

½-inch piece of fresh turmeric
    root, peeled

ice cubes (optional)

**SERVES 1—2**

Make sure the beet, tomatoes and carrot are washed thoroughly. Blend all the ingredients except the ice cubes in a high-powered blender on high for 2–3 minutes until smooth.

Serve immediately, with some ice cubes if you like, for a fresh, chilled smoothie.

*Raw Beets*

Beets are a brilliant liver cleanser. The liver is responsible for filtering the blood and is one of your frontline defences against harmful toxins and chemicals. Given this heavy workload, it's good to take care of your liver when you can by consuming liver-function-boosting foods.

raw breakfasts

raw cake

# Mango & Macadamia Smoothie

Mangos are so uplifting, they're believed to clear the skin and refresh the body from the inside out. This smoothie is literally happiness in a glass; we'll drink it any time of day if we're feeling a little bit low and want something indulgent but light.

1 medium-large mango,
    peeled, pitted and chopped
1 banana
1 cup almond or other
    nut milk
½ cup macadamia nuts
1 tablespoon hemp or pea
    protein powder
¾ teaspoon vanilla powder

SERVES 1—2

Blend all the ingredients together in a high-powered blender on high until smooth. If you prefer a runnier smoothie, add a dash of water. Serve immediately.

43

*Macadamia Nuts*
Rich in monounsaturated fatty acids, creamy macadamia nuts have a waxy texture and a buttery taste, making them perfectly suited to raw desserts and indulgent smoothies.

# Berry & Schisandra Bowl

If you wake up feeling foggy, this zingy bowl can really cut through the mist. Berries are generally rich in antioxidants, while schisandra is known for being a bit of a beauty tonic as it's thought to protect the skin from sun and wind exposure, allergic reactions and environmental stress. Eat this if you want to be wide awake and looking fine.

2 cups mixed berries (we used
    strawberries, raspberries,
    blueberries)
¾ cup nut milk (we used
    almond)
½ cup pumpkin seeds
⅓ cup cashews
½ tablespoon pea or hemp
    protein powder
½ teaspoon schisandra powder
handful of ice cubes

For the topping (optional)
your favorite fruit, diced (we
    used dragon fruit)
sprinkling of RAWnola
    (see page 56)

**SERVES 1—2**

Place all the ingredients except the toppings into a high-powered blender and blend on high until the mixture is as smooth as possible.

Pour the mixture into a serving bowl or divide between two individual bowls. If you like, top with whatever fruit you have available and a sprinkling of RAWnola for added crunch.

*Schisandra*
Schisandra has been used in traditional Chinese medicine for over 2,000 years. Known as an adaptogenic berry, it is completely nontoxic and helps to reduce stress. It also helps with overall vitality and is used within Chinese medicine in prolonging life, slowing the aging process, increasing energy, fighting fatigue, protecting the liver and as a sexual tonic. It is also a significant source of antioxidants and has been shown to possess anti-inflammatory qualities.

44

# Beet & Strawberry Overnight Oats

If you've got an early morning start or an important day ahead of you, this is the perfect recipe to prepare in advance to give yourself a head start and make sure you are fueled up when you need it the most. Beets are a great source of a number of vitamins and minerals, and are particularly supportive of the liver's detoxification process (see page 40). Decant this into a sealable jar and devour.

one-quarter of a medium beet

1 cup chopped strawberries, plus more for serving if desired

½ cup almond milk, plus more for serving

1 cup gluten-free rolled oats (we use sprouted)

½ tablespoon chia seeds

honey or coconut syrup, to taste

SERVES 1–2

Make sure the beet is washed thoroughly. Juice the beet and half of the chopped strawberries in a high-powered juicer on high. Pour the juice into a bowl, add the almond milk and oats and stir until the oats are fully submerged in the liquid.

Add the chia seeds to the bowl and stir in to ensure they're covered. Throw in the remaining chopped strawberries and a drizzle of honey to taste, stir, then cover with a lid or plastic wrap and place in the fridge overnight.

We like to add another splash of almond milk and a squeeze of honey before eating in the morning, along with a few fresh chopped strawberries.

45

raw cake

# Banana & Peanut Butter Smoothie Bowl

Never trust anyone who doesn't like peanut butter. Banana and PB were born to be together. This is a wonderfully thick and creamy smoothie that will have you wondering how on earth it can be good for you. The baobab and lucuma are optional additions, but they will enhance the nutritional benefits of this smoothie (and your day), while the peanut butter and hemp seeds combine to form a perfect source of protein.

1½ ripe bananas

¾ cup almond milk

2 tablespoons peanut butter (or another nut butter if you don't eat peanuts)

1 tablespoon shelled hemp seeds

1 tablespoon golden flax seeds

½ tablespoon baobab powder (optional)

½ tablespoon lucuma powder (optional)

½ tablespoon bee pollen, for serving (see note on safe use on page 181)

SERVES 1—2

Slice the half banana into rounds and set aside. Place the whole banana and all the rest of the ingredients except the bee pollen in a high-powered blender and blend on high until creamy and smooth.

Pour the mixture into a serving bowl or divide between two individual bowls. Decorate with the banana slices and a sprinkling of bee pollen if using.

47

# Power
# Balls

When energy balls first cropped up we loved trying them, then we noticed that the mass-market products were full of ingredients that were not as appealing as their springy names suggested. So we started to make our own, packing in as many nutrients and superfoods as we could. These days we take it a step further, making balls that are specific to certain needs. We've designed these with three purposes in mind – to help immunity, aid brain function, and encourage radiant skin. If you don't have all of the superfoods, just use whatever you do have. The beauty of these balls is that you can freestyle – as long as you taste-test in order to balance the flavors.

## Beauty Balls

These bites contain many of the beneficial ingredients that are believed to keep you looking and feeling good and healthy from the inside out. Brazil nuts are a source of selenium, which fights against free radicals thought to cause premature aging, as do sunflower seeds with their vitamin E; these and camu camu also help to fight acne and maintain healthy skin. Goji berries provide antioxidants, and collagen helps in the battle against the appearance of aging. These balls are bouncing with beauty benefits!

½ cup Brazil nuts
¼ cup hulled sunflower seeds
¼ cup goji berries
½ tablespoon collagen powder
zest of 1 orange
½ tablespoon camu camu
  powder
2 tablespoons maple syrup or
  other liquid natural sweetener

**MAKES 12 BALLS**

---

Place all the ingredients except the maple syrup in a high-powered food processor and blend on high until fine. Add the syrup and blend again until the mixture sticks together. If it needs help sticking, add a splash of water – no more than 1 tablespoon.

Scoop out 12 equal measures of the mixture with a tablespoon and roll each into a ball. Place on a plate or baking pan lined with parchment paper and leave in the fridge for 1–2 hours. When firm, store in a sealed container in the fridge for up to 1 week.

**raw cake**

*Above:* Beauty Balls (green), Immunity Balls (red), Brain Balls (yellow)

# Immunity Balls

These have been designed using ingredients that will help build and maintain a healthy immune system. Brazil nuts are rich in selenium, which is essential to enable your white blood cells to fight infection. Cashews and maple syrup are a good source of zinc, which is vital for your body's immune response. Ginger has been found to have anti-microbial properties, and may help in the fight against free radicals. Turmeric is a powerful antioxidant with an active ingredient called curcumin that has been investigated for its anti-viral and anti-fungal properties, as is bee pollen. Lemon is high in vitamin C, adding a little immunity boost.

½ cup Brazil nuts
½ cup almonds
¼ cup cashews
1 teaspoon bee pollen (see note on safe use on page 181)
zest of 1 lemon
½ teaspoon Siberian ginseng
½ teaspoon freshly grated ginger root
¼ teaspoon turmeric powder
2 tablespoons maple syrup
2 tablespoons lemon juice

50

**MAKES 12 BALLS**

Blend all the ingredients except the maple syrup and lemon juice in a high-powered food processor on high until fine. Add the maple syrup and lemon juice and blend again until the mixture sticks together well.

Using a tablespoon, scoop out 12 equal measures of the mixture and roll each into a ball with your hands. Place them on a plate or baking pan lined with parchment paper and leave in the fridge for 1–2 hours.

When firm, transfer the balls to a sealed container and store in the fridge for up to 1 week.

# Brain Balls

We designed these to help fight that brain fog – when you're sitting at your desk trying to concentrate yet you find yourself 100 miles away from the task at hand.

Pecans contain copper, which we need to make norepinephrine, a neurotransmitter that your brain cells use to communicate. Research has suggested that antioxidants and other beneficial compounds in walnuts may help to counteract age-related cognitive decline, and even reduce the risk of Alzheimer's. Pumpkin seeds are rich in zinc that is valuable for optimizing memory and thinking power. Hemp seeds are full of good fats that are essential components of a healthy brain. Bee pollen has a high amino acid content that helps to keep the memory functional and the mind alert. Chlorella and spirulina provide vitamins, minerals, omega-3 fatty acids and amino acids, which are essential in supporting brain function. Wheatgrass is found to be high in vitamin K and folates, which support brain cell growth and memory. American ginseng is believed to lower stress levels and help keep the memory sharp.

⅔ cup pecans

⅓ cup walnuts

2 tablespoons pumpkin seeds

2 tablespoons shelled hemp seeds

1 teaspoon bee pollen (see note on safe use on page 181)

1 teaspoon chia seeds

½ teaspoon chlorella powder

½ teaspoon spirulina powder

½ teaspoon wheatgrass powder

½ teaspoon American ginseng powder

2 tablespoons coconut syrup or other liquid natural sweetener

**MAKES 12 BALLS**

---

Place all the ingredients except the coconut syrup in a high-powered food processor and blend on high until fine and even. Add the coconut syrup and blend again until the mixture sticks together well. If it needs help sticking together, add a small splash of water – no more than 1 tablespoon.

Using a tablespoon, scoop out 12 equal measures of the mixture and roll each into a ball with your hands. Place them on a plate or baking pan lined with parchment paper and leave in the fridge for 1–2 hours.

When firm, transfer the balls to a sealed container and store in the fridge for up to 1 week.

# Lemon
# Tulsi Balls

We love the freshness of the lemon juice in these balls, cutting through the sweet flavors and complementing the spiciness of tulsi. And if you need any more reasons to make these balls, check out the benefits of tulsi, the queen of herbs, on page 186.

½ cup cashews
½ cup almonds
½ cup desiccated coconut
½ cup pitted Medjool dates
¾ cup lemon juice
½ tablespoon tulsi powder
zest of 1 lemon

**MAKES 10 BALLS**

---

Place the cashews, almonds and desiccated coconut in a high-powered food processor and blend on high just until coarsely chopped – you don't want these too fine. Add the dates and blend again quickly to combine. Then chuck in the lemon juice, tulsi powder and lemon zest and blend until the mixture sticks together and forms a ball.

Using a tablespoon, scoop out 10 equal measures of the mixture and roll each into a ball with your hands. Place them on a plate or baking pan lined with parchment paper and leave in the fridge for 1–2 hours.

When firm, transfer the balls to a sealed container and store in the fridge for up to 1 week.

# Flat #42 Swiss Bircher Muesli

This staple was created by our old apartment mate, James, at the notorious warehouse Flat 42 in Dalston. We became obsessed with this simple overnight time-saver and we still eat it in the spring and summer months when making porridge just seems a bit out of place.

1 cup gluten-free rolled oats
¾ cup almond or other nut milk,
   plus more as needed
juice of 1 orange
one-quarter of an apple, thinly
   sliced
¼ cup raisins
coconut nectar, to your taste
   (or honey if you are not vegan)
zest of 1 lemon
sprinkle of ground cinnamon

SERVES 1

Combine the oats, nut milk and orange juice in a medium bowl, mixing well with a spoon. Cover and leave to soak overnight in the fridge.

The next morning, give the mixture a good stir and add a drop more almond milk if the muesli is too dry.

Spoon into a bowl and dot with the apple slices, sprinkle with raisins, add a squeeze of coconut nectar and finally sprinkle on the lemon zest and cinnamon. (Too good to be true.)

53

raw cake

# Hardihood RAWnola Clusters

For the days when you just can't deny yourself a bowl of cereal for breakfast, do it the grown-up way with raw granola drowned in ice-cold nut milk. We've actually been known to eat this for lunch, dinner, supper and a midnight snack too.

1 cup gluten-free rolled oats (we used sprouted)

½ cup raw whole buckwheat groats (we used sprouted)

½ cup almonds

½ cup pecans

½ cup cashews

¼ cup raisins

¼ cup pumpkin seeds

3 tablespoons coconut flakes

2 tablespoons shelled hemp seeds

1 tablespoon maca powder

¼ teaspoon ground cinnamon

generous pinch of Himalayan salt

3 tablespoons coconut oil, melted

3 tablespoons maple syrup or coconut syrup

SERVES 4

Preheat the oven to no higher than 110°F or to its nearest low temperature.

Blend the oats in a high-powered food processor on high until they become fine, and then add all the remaining ingredients except the coconut oil and maple syrup. Pulse until the nuts and seeds are broken up but remain chunky.

Place the mixture in a large mixing bowl and pour in the coconut oil and maple syrup. Mix together with your hands, making sure that all of the dry ingredients are covered. Squash together with your fingers, creating some clumps.

Tip the mixture onto a baking pan lined with parchment paper, push the crumbly mixture together and pat it down so that it sticks together as much as possible. Place in the oven for 3 hours, or until the mixture has dried out.

When it has dehydrated, leave it to rest for 10–15 minutes before breaking it up into clusters and storing it in a sealed jar, where it will keep for 1 week.

*TIP:* To sprout your own buckwheat for this recipe, cover it in water for 30 minutes, then rinse and drain. You can mix it right in, it will dehydrate when the RAWnola is in the oven.

55

# Raw Banana Pancakes

This is a raw, light take on the small American pancake that we all love in the UK. Eat them stacked with layers of coconut yogurt and berries: You will feel like you've had a sumptuous treat. *(Pictured on pages 58-59.)*

2 tablespoons flax seeds
½ cup pecans
¼ cup buckwheat flour
1 banana
½ cup almond milk
¼ teaspoon ground cinnamon
pinch of Himalayan salt
coconut yogurt and fresh
    berries, for serving

**MAKES ABOUT 12 PANCAKES**

Preheat the oven to no higher than 110°F or to its nearest low temperature.

Grind the flax seeds in a high-powered food processor until fine like flour, then transfer them to a bowl and stir in 3 tablespoons of water. Leave for 10–15 minutes to swell; this turns them into an egg substitute.

Grind the pecans in the clean food processor until they are fine like flour, add buckwheat flour, banana, almond milk, cinnamon and salt and blend until the mixture becomes slightly runny, a little less wet than your usual pancake batter. Place large spoonfuls of the batter onto a plate or baking pan lined with parchment paper and smooth into round pancake shapes.

Place in the oven for roughly 1 hour, or until the tops of the pancakes look dried out. Cover the pancakes with another sheet of parchment paper and flip the papers over so that the dried pancake tops are now facing down. Leave in the oven to dehydrate for a further 30 minutes–1 hour or until the bases of the pancakes (now flipped to the top) are dry enough for you to peel off the paper. If they are dry, take them out of the oven and let them cool on the side before stacking with coconut yogurt and berries.

# Berry & Ginger Chia Seed Jam

We love this recipe. It reminds us of jam-sandwich picnics in the park. It's hugely versatile: if ginger isn't your thing, add a sprinkle of fresh thyme to the mix or swap our fruit for blueberries, blackberries or figs. *(Pictured on page 58.)*

1½ cups mixed berries (we used strawberries and raspberries)
½-inch piece of fresh ginger root, peeled and diced
2 tablespoons rice malt syrup or other liquid natural sweetener, plus more to taste
2 tablespoons chia seeds

**MAKES 1 JAR**

Place the berries and ginger in a high-powered food processor and blend on high to your preferred texture – if you like smooth jam, blend it for a little longer, but if you like a few lumps, stop when there are still small chunks remaining. Add the rice malt syrup and chia seeds, stirring by hand until everything is incorporated, and adding a little more syrup, if you like.

Transfer to a clean jar or container, cover with a lid and leave in the fridge to set for no less than 1 hour. This will keep for up to 5 days in the fridge.

57

> *Chia Seeds*
> A brilliant source of soluble fiber and omega-3s, chia seeds have a gel-like texture once soaked, making them perfect for helping raw puddings and fruity treats set.

# Knockdown Ginger

We love to start the day with a fresh hit of live nutrients. This juice will leave you feeling alert, hydrated and energized. The yellow beet has all the benefits of traditional beets minus the intense purple color. If you can't find the yellow variety, a regular red beet will work perfectly.

4 handfuls of spinach

4 lacinato kale leaves

1 yellow beet

one-quarter of a large cucumber

half an apple, cored

1 lemon, peeled

half a medium-hot chili

1-inch piece of fresh ginger root, peeled

½-inch piece of fresh turmeric root, peeled

SERVES 1–2

Put all the ingredients in a juicer, juice, pour into a glass or divide between two glasses and enjoy!

60

> **Lacinato Kale**
> Also known as Tuscan black cabbage and cavolo nero, this leafy green is rich in iron and calcium and at its sweetest and most tender in autumn and winter.

raw breakfasts

*Above:* Spicy Immunity Shot (top), Adaptogenic Energy Tonic (middle right), Glowing Skin Tonic (bottom)

# Glowing Skin Tonic

If you live in a fast-paced city with its inevitable pollution, do what you can to turn the lights up from the inside. This tried-and-tested complexion brightener fits the bill.

1 pink grapefruit, peeled
1 cup raspberries
1 cup coconut water
leaves from 2 mint sprigs
½ teaspoon collagen powder
½ teaspoon probiotic powder
½ teaspoon pearl powder
   (optional)
handful of ice cubes, for
   serving

SERVES 1–2

Juice the grapefruit in a juicer.

Meanwhile, throw the raspberries and coconut water into a high-powered blender and blend on high until totally smooth. Add the mint leaves, grapefruit juice and the collagen, probiotic and pearl powders and blend again until the mint has broken down.

Pour into a glass or divide between two glasses, chuck in the ice and serve.

63

# Spicy Immunity Shot

This drink will blow your socks off and support your immune system in one fell swoop. We'll concoct this at the slightest sign of a sniffle. With lemon for alkalizing, turmeric for inflammation, ginger root for stomach settling, apple cider vinegar as a natural antibiotic and mucus remover, echinacea for immunity, astragulus for flu symptoms and chili for metabolism, there isn't a single ingredient packed in here that doesn't serve a purpose.

1 lemon, peeled

2-inch piece of fresh ginger root, peeled

½-inch piece of fresh turmeric root, peeled

one-quarter of a medium-hot chili (seeds and all)

1 rosemary sprig

1 teaspoon apple cider vinegar

10 drops liquid echinacea (optional)

½ teaspoon astragalus powder (optional)

**SERVES 1—2**

---

Place the lemon, ginger, turmeric, chili and rosemary into a juicer and juice.

Add the vinegar to the juice along with the echinacea and astragalus, if using, stirring until combined.

Pour into a glass or divide between two glasses and down it in one.

# Adaptogenic Energy Tonic

A punchy and flavorsome drink that will keep you feeling energized throughout your day. The addition of the optional adaptogenic superfoods in this recipe will be a huge boost to your energy levels, focus and vibrancy, especially if consumed on a regular basis.

1 carrot

half a medium beet

1 lemon, peeled

½-inch piece of fresh ginger root, peeled

½-inch piece of fresh turmeric root, peeled

½ teaspoon American ginseng powder (optional)

½ teaspoon Siberian ginseng powder (optional)

½ teaspoon astragalus powder (optional)

SERVES 1–2

Make sure the carrot and beet are washed thoroughly, then juice in a high-powered juicer. Add all the remaining ingredients and juice again – if they aren't combining well and the mixture is lumpy, use a small hand whisk to combine.

*Ginseng*
American ginseng is an adaptogen – an herb that helps the body adapt to stress. It can have a positive impact on a wide range of health problems, and help maintain overall health and vitality. It is also said to help with memory loss.

Siberian ginseng is known to be an energizer, which helps protect the adrenal glands, increasing their capacity to withstand prolonged stress, which in turn helps fight fatigue and anxiety. It also helps to maintain healthy blood circulation, dispersing oxygen and other nutrients efficiently around the body and brain.

65

# Immunity Hot Chocolate

For centuries the Incas and Mayans, ancient civilizations of South America, swore by the healing properties of chocolate, and still today their claims cannot be denied. When heated this elixir becomes extra creamy, like a hug in a mug. Be prepared to fall in love with everything and everyone around you.

1 cup almond or other
   dairy-free milk
2 tablespoons coconut nectar
   or other natural sweetener
1½ tablespoons cacao powder
1 teaspoon coconut oil
½-inch piece of fresh ginger
   root, peeled
½-inch piece of fresh
   turmeric root, peeled
1 tablespoon chaga powder
   (optional)
ground cinnamon, for
   sprinkling

**SERVES 2**

Place all the ingredients except the cinnamon in a high-powered blender and blend on high until the ginger and turmeric have broken down completely.

Serve cold as a shake or warmed in a saucepan; for either way, sprinkle some cinnamon over each serving. You'll enjoy a heart-opening, immunity-boosting, night-on-the-sofa elixir.

# Nut Another Smoothie Bowl

We start the day with this chilled-out alternative to porridge when we want warming spices and comforting banana without the heat.

1½ bananas, frozen
½ cup mixed nuts, such as Brazil, almonds, cashews
¼ cup gluten-free rolled oats (we used sprouted)
½ cup almond or other nut milk
1 teaspoon coconut sugar
1 teaspoon lucuma powder
½ teaspoon probiotic powder
¼ teaspoon ground cinnamon
pinch of Himalayan salt
¾ cup filtered water

For the topping (optional)
chopped strawberries
ground cinnamon
your favorite seeds (we love pumpkin, hemp and golden flax seeds)

SERVES 1—2

Blend all the ingredients together in a high-powered blender on high, adding the water last, a little at a time, until the smoothie is your preferred consistency.

Pour into a bowl and serve, scattered with your preferred toppings if you like.

67

### Probiotic Powder

Probiotics are live bacteria and yeasts that benefit our gut health. Known as "good bacteria," they help to balance our digestive system, process some forms of fiber and may help to keep our bowel function regular. The different strains of bacteria have varying effects; they can produce a number of vitamins, including B6 and B12, aid in the absorption of various minerals and can help to treat diarrhea.

# Matcha Mint Iced Cooler

A refreshing, energizing, achingly cool cooler, we love to enjoy this in the garden at our studio. It's the perfect summertime hydrating drink with the uplifting benefits of matcha thrown in.

juice of 1 orange
6-8 fresh mint leaves
½ tablespoon matcha powder
juice of half a lemon
3 cups (750 ml) sparkling
  water
ice cubes, for serving

SERVES 2—4

---

Pour the orange juice into a high-powered blender and add the mint leaves and matcha powder. Blend until the leaves start to break down, then pour into a medium decanter, stirring in the lemon juice and sparkling water.

Pour over ice to serve.

*Matcha*
A powdered green tea – far more potent than regular green tea – matcha contains high quantities of polyphenol compounds (catechins), antioxidants that are said to have anticarcinogenic properties. Its bitter flavor can be overwhelming, so use it sparingly.

raw breakfasts

raw cake

# Anti-inflammatory Golden Milk

We've come to learn that inflammation in one form or another is at the root of many bodily ailments. Turmeric is one of nature's powerful anti-inflammatory wonders and should help to counteract this, keeping you feeling light, clear-headed and energized, while the addition of black pepper helps the blood to better absorb the curcumin from the turmeric.

1 cup almonds, soaked
  overnight
1 cup pumpkin seeds, soaked
  overnight
2 cups filtered water
¼ cup pitted soft dates
1-inch piece of fresh turmeric
  root, peeled, or use 3
  tablespoons ground if you
  can't get fresh
½ teaspoon vanilla powder
pinch of ground black pepper

SERVES 2–4

Drain the almonds and pumpkin seeds, rinse under cold running water, drain again and place in a high-powered blender along with all the other ingredients. Blend on high until as smooth as possible.

Pour the mixture through a nut milk bag into a large bowl or measuring cup. Squeeze the bag to make sure that all the liquid comes through and discard the pulp left in the bag.

71

Pour the milk into a clean bottle or jar and refrigerate until ready to serve. This will keep for 2–3 days in the fridge.

# Shroom Shake

Sorry to disappoint, this ain't that kind of mushroom shake. No full moon parties here...

Medicinal mushrooms have been on our radar for a few years now, but it is only recently that we've noticed them creeping their way onto more shop shelves. Powerful adaptogens (see page 180), they should be used sparingly but often for optimal results. This shake is smooth and delicious, with a whole host of benefits.

1 cup homemade nut milk
(see pages 21–25)
1 teaspoon coconut oil
1 teaspoon coconut sugar,
or to taste, (optional)
½ teaspoon chaga powder
½ teaspoon reishi powder
½ teaspoon cordyceps
powder
½ teaspoon ground
cinnamon

**SERVES 2**

Add all the ingredients to a small saucepan and heat gently, whisking until all are well combined and the shake is nicely warmed. Pour into a mug or glass and enjoy.

*TIP:* Don't worry if you only have one variety of these mushrooms – just adjust the amount of the one you are using. Feel free to include any Chinese medicinal mushrooms for a powerful healing shake.

# Brown Rice Horchata

We'd been lusting after horchata from afar for some time, and it wasn't until we got to LA that we first tasted the Mexican real deal. This recipe originates from a plant-based alternative to the nut-based classic that blew our minds; the addition of lucuma gives it that extra spark and the cinnamon stick really adds depth of flavor.

1 cup brown rice
1 quart (4 cups) filtered water
1 cinnamon stick
1 cup almond or other
  non-dairy milk
¼ cup maple syrup
1 tablespoon lucuma powder
  (optional)
½ teaspoon vanilla powder
½ teaspoon ground cinnamon
ice cubes, for serving

**SERVES 2—4**

Put the rice in a bowl or jar with the water and cinnamon stick, cover with a cloth or tea towel and leave to soak at room temperature overnight.

The next day, remove the cinnamon stick and blend the rice with the water in a high-powered blender. Pour through a nut milk bag into a bowl, squeezing out all of the liquid; discard the rice in the bag. Return the liquid to a clean blender; add all the other ingredients except the ice and pulse to combine.

Serve the over ice. This will keep in the fridge for 3 days.

73

Chapter 3

**Most days we are** constantly on the go, and sometimes we just need a hit of something lovely to help us along. We love making these fun indulgent treats. They can be eaten at your leisure, whether you're on the go or making repeated visits to the fridge. Get your friends involved in whipping up a batch, or make them with your children, but take it easy on the bowl-licking when you're using cacao – that stuff's dynamite: There has been many an occasion where we have been found giggling and bouncing off the ceilings after getting high from too much quality control!

# The Modern Scone

This is a modern, raw take on a traditional English favorite. Our mums, Ingrid and Rachel, love these scones, so they come with the mothers' seal of approval. They are a must for any revitalized afternoon tea menu. *(Pictured on pages 74–75.)*

## For the scones
3 cups gluten-free rolled oats
2 cups cashews
½ cup coconut sugar
¼ cup raisins
1 tablespoon lucuma powder
  (optional)
generous pinch of Himalayan
  salt
¼–½ cup nut milk (we used
  almond)
juice and zest of 1 lemon
Berry & Chia Seed Jam (see
  page 57), for serving

## For the coconut cream
1 cup coconut butter
2 tablespoons coconut syrup

**MAKES 7—8 SCONES**

Preheat the oven to no higher than 110°F or to its nearest low temperature.

Place the oats and cashews in a high-powered food processor and blend on high to make a fine flour. Pour into a large mixing bowl and stir in the coconut sugar, raisins, lucuma and salt.

Pour the nut milk into the mixture, a little at a time, then the lemon juice and zest and knead the dough with your hands until well combined. Separate into 7 or 8 small balls, and place on a baking sheet. Dehydrate in the oven for 3–4 hours or until the outside is dry. Remove from the oven and leave to rest for 10 minutes.

For the coconut cream, add the coconut butter and coconut syrup to the clean food processor and blend until smooth.

Split the scones and serve with the coconut cream and some Berry & Chia Seed Jam.

77

# Banana Dough Bites

Smooth, creamy maca takes these outrageously good dough bites to the next level. Keep in the fridge or store in a recycled jam jar for rich pickings on the move.

### For the chocolate mix
½ cup cacao butter, melted
¼ cup melted coconut oil, plus
   more as needed
¼ cup rice malt syrup
¾ cup cacao powder

### For the dough
1½ cups cashews
¼ cup gluten-free rolled oats
¾ cup coconut sugar
one-quarter of a medium
   banana
3 tablespoons maca powder
3 tablespoons rice malt syrup
1 tablespoon melted coconut oil
½ teaspoon vanilla powder
large pinch of salt

**MAKES 10—12 BITES**

First make the chocolate mix. Combine all the ingredients for the chocolate in a high-powered food processor on high. If the mixture isn't runny enough, add a little more coconut oil until you get the perfect dipping consistency. Pour a small puddle of the chocolate mix (around 3 tablespoons) onto a sheet of parchment paper and transfer to the freezer for about 10 minutes to set. Set aside the rest of the chocolate mix.

Next, start the dough. Blitz the nuts and oats in the clean food processor until fine, then add all other ingredients and blend until the mixture has a doughy texture. Transfer to a large bowl.

Remove the chocolate from the freezer once it has set and crumble it into pieces. Drop these chips into the dough and mix quickly – they may get a little melty, but that's fine. Place the dough in the freezer for 10 minutes as a whole block to cool off, then take it out and roll it into medium balls, placing the balls on a plate lined with parchment paper.

Dip and roll the balls in the reserved dipping chocolate and place them back on the parchment paper using a spoon or fork. Place in the fridge to set for 1 hour – then devour. We challenge you to eat only one!

raw treats

# Raw Hot Cross Buns

We're not religious, but we'll worship at the church of these buns any day. It's always fun to recreate the classics without using traditional techniques and these were a real breakthrough. Oozing with exactly the same crunch and flavors as the traditional hot cross bun that you know and love, these nutritionally balanced treats are bunderful.

### For the cashew cream cross
1½ cups cashews, soaked for
   1–2 hours , rinsed and drained
juice of 1 lemon
3 tablespoons rice malt syrup
   or other natural liquid
   sweetener
½ teaspoon vanilla powder

### For the buns
1 cup pitted dates, soaked
   for 5 minutes to soften
1 cup almonds
1 cup gluten-free rolled oats
2 tablespoons maca powder
½ teaspoon vanilla powder
½ teaspoon ground cinnamon
½ teaspoon ground ginger
zest of 1 orange
3 generous pinches of
   Himalayan salt
¾ cup raisins

**MAKES 6 BUNS**

Preheat the oven to no higher than 110°F or to its nearest low temperature.

First make the cashew cream. Blend all the ingredients in a high-powered blender – we used a Vitamix to get this ultra-smooth. Transfer the cream to a piping bag and put in the fridge to firm for 2–3 hours.

Meanwhile, make the buns. Blend all the ingredients except the raisins with 3 tablespoons of water in a high-powered food processor for 2–3 minutes until the mixture has a dough-like consistency. Transfer the dough to a bowl and mix the raisins in by hand. Shape the dough into 6 balls and place on a baking sheet, spacing slightly apart and squashing down slightly. Cut a cross shape into the top of each bun.

Put the buns in the oven for 1–2 hours to dehydrate. Remove from the oven and leave to cool.

Once cool, pipe the cashew cream into the cross indentations on top of the buns and eat!

80

# Cacao Chaga Doughnuts

We love this recipe because it's an all-round crowd pleaser. Inspired by the chocolate doughnuts of your dreams, here the uplifting effects of cacao and the added benefits of chaga make for one powerfully packed, sumptuous doughnut experience. Dunk in chocolate or leave them baring all, the choice is yours. *(Pictured on pages 84-85.)*

### For the doughnuts

1½ cups gluten-free rolled oats

½ cup walnuts

½ cup almonds

¼ cup hulled sunflower seeds

2 tablespoons chia seeds

⅓ cup coconut sugar

¼ cup cacao powder

1 tablespoon chaga powder

½ teaspoon ground cinnamon

½ teaspoon vanilla powder

2 large pinches of salt

½ cup melted coconut oil

⅓ cup rice malt syrup, plus more if needed

### For decorating (optional)

Raw Chocolate (see page 26)

fresh flower petals, crushed nuts or desiccated coconut

**MAKES 18 MINI DOUGHNUTS
OR YOU CAN MIX SMALL AND LARGE SIZES**

Preheat the oven to no higher than 110°F or to its nearest low temperature.

Place the oats, nuts, sunflower seeds and chia seeds in a high-powered food processor and blend on high until as smooth as possible. Blend in the rest of the ingredients, adding the coconut oil and rice malt syrup last. Once the mixture is blended, make sure it is sticky enough and doesn't crumble apart – if it does, add another squirt of syrup.

Press the mixture into the doughnut molds of your choice – we used a mixture of small and large molds. Place in the oven for 2–3 hours, or until the doughnuts have dried out slightly. Remove from the oven and leave to cool on a wire rack, if needed, for 10–15 minutes.

The doughnuts will keep for up to 5 days, undecorated, in the fridge. If you like, when ready to eat, drizzle or dunk the doughnuts into Raw Chocolate, sprinkle with petals, nuts or desiccated coconut (see pages 178–179 for topping inspiration) and place in the fridge until the chocolate hardens.

82

# Matcha Pistachio Doughnuts

These matcha doughnuts became instant legends among our studio mates, who regularly get to sample our creations. Being on the more savory side of sweet, these are great any time of day and pack an added punch in the form of the deliciously mellow matcha. Matcha + doughnuts equal a winning combo. *(Pictured on pages 84–85.)*

### For the doughnuts
1½ cups gluten-free rolled oats

1 cup cashews

½ cup desiccated coconut

2 tablespoons matcha powder

generous pinch of Himalayan salt

generous ½ cup rice malt syrup

¼ cup shelled and finely chopped pistachios

### For decorating (optional)
Raw Chocolate (see page 26) or coconut cream (see page 77)

a few shelled and chopped pistachios

**MAKES 18 MINI DOUGHNUTS OR YOU CAN MIX SMALL AND LARGE SIZES**

Preheat the oven to no higher than 110°F or to its nearest low temperature.

Place the oats, cashews and desiccated coconut in a high-powered food processor and blend on high until fine. Throw in all the remaining ingredients except the pistachios and blend until well combined and sticky.

Divide the finely chopped pistachios into the bottom of the doughnut molds (we used some big rings and some small). Then press the dough into the molds on top of the pistachios and place in the oven for 3–4 hours, or until the doughnuts have dried out slightly. Remove from the oven, remove from the molds and place on a wire rack to cool completely.

The doughnuts will keep for up to 5 days, undecorated, in the fridge. If you like, when ready to eat, decorate the doughnuts by dipping the tops in Raw Chocolate or piping on some coconut cream and sprinkling with chopped pistachios.

83

raw cake

# Beet Red Velvet Cupcakes

This is one of our favorite throwbacks: It's a nod to our teens, when red velvet cupcakes were the rage. We've brought the recipe totally up-to-date in this raw interpretation.

## For the cupcakes

1 cup almonds

½ cup cashews

2 cups grated beets (wash them first!)

¾ cup coconut sugar

½ cup pitted Medjool dates

½ teaspoon vanilla powder

## For the coconut frosting

1½ cups desiccated coconut, soaked for at least 1 hour in ¼ cup filtered water

¼ cup rice malt syrup

¼ cup melted coconut oil

MAKES 8–10 CUPCAKES

First make the cupcakes. Place the almonds and cashews in a high-powered food processor and blend on high until they become fine like flour. Add the remaining ingredients to the food processor and blend until smooth.

Arrange 8–10 cupcake liners on a baking pan. Spoon the mixture into them and transfer to the freezer for 30 minutes until firm.

Meanwhile, make the frosting. Add the soaked desiccated coconut, rice malt syrup and coconut oil to a high-powered blender. Blend until absolutely smooth and then blend some more – this will be what turns the frosting light and fluffy!

Transfer the frosting to a piping bag fitted with a wide tip. Swirl the frosting atop the cupcakes and then place them in the fridge for 1–2 hours to set. They will keep in the fridge for up to 5 days.

87

# Raspberry Peanut Butter Cups

Our dads first introduced us to the delights of peanut butter and jam on toast, so we suppose it's fair to say that these raspberry peanut butter cups are Dad-inspired. Downright delicious, these definitely keep the PBJ dream alive.

### For the chocolate mixture
1 cup cacao oil, melted
¾ cup cacao powder
¾ cup rice malt syrup or
    other liquid natural sweetener
¼ cup cacao butter, melted

### For the peanut butter filling
½ cup peanut butter (use the
    no-added-sugar natural
    variety)
¼ cup coconut sugar
¼ cup rice malt syrup or
    other liquid natural sweetener
¼ cup melted coconut oil
raspberries, whole or cut
    in half, to decorate

**MAKES 20—25 CUP TREATS**

Place all the chocolate mixture ingredients in a high-powered food processor and blend on high until well combined (try not to overmix). Transfer to a squeeze bottle, or a bowl if you don't have one.

Place all of the peanut butter filling ingredients except the raspberries in a medium bowl and stir together until smooth.

To assemble, arrange 20—25 mini cupcake liners on a platter that will fit into your fridge (or use molds). Divide roughly half the chocolate mixture equally between the liners. Place the platter in the fridge for 15—20 minutes until firm.

Spoon a dollop of the peanut butter filling into each of the liners, on top of the chocolate mixture, smoothing it out with a spoon. Press half a raspberry flat on top of each or place a whole raspberry upright.

Divide the remaining chocolate mixture into each filled liner, covering the raspberry and peanut butter. (The upright raspberries will poke through the chocolate nicely.) Place back into the fridge for 20—30 minutes more before serving. Having only one will be your problem…

88

**raw cake**

raw treats

# Banana Loaf & Cream Frosting

We were both born and raised on banana bread, so it only made sense to recreate our childhood favorite. This is just as heartwarming as the one Grandma used to make, only raw and enhanced with the benefits of natural nutrients. Dollop on the deliciously creamy frosting generously.

## For the loaf

coconut oil, for greasing

1 cup pecans

1 cup whole walnuts, plus ¾ cup coarsely chopped

1 cup gluten-free rolled oats

1 cup pitted, coarsely chopped dates

4 small ripe bananas

¼ cup coconut sugar

2 tablespoons rice malt syrup or other natural liquid sweetener

1 tablespoon ground ginger

pinch of salt

## For the cream frosting

1 small banana

one 14-ounce (400 ml) can coconut milk, refrigerated overnight; use the top layer of cream only

2 tablespoons rice malt syrup

**SERVES 8—10**

Preheat the oven to no higher than 110°F or to its nearest low temperature. Line a 5- by 7-inch loaf pan with parchment paper and rub the sides with coconut oil.

First make the loaf. Place the pecans, the 1 cup whole walnuts and the oats in a high-powered food processor and blend on high until they form a flour-like consistency. Transfer to a large mixing bowl. Stir in the dates and two-thirds of the chopped walnuts (reserve the rest for sprinkling over the frosting) and set aside.

Add the bananas to the food processor and blend on high until smooth, then tip in the coconut sugar, rice malt syrup, ginger and salt, and blend again. Stir the banana mixture into the dry ingredients until completely combined. Press into the prepared pan and dehydrate in the oven for 3 hours.

Meanwhile, make the cream frosting. Blend the banana in the clean food processor. Scoop the layer of cream on the top of the watery coconut milk into the processor; add rice malt syrup and blend again for a few seconds. Transfer to a bowl and place in the fridge for 2–3 hours until the frosting stiffens.

To assemble, take the loaf out of the pan and let it rest for 30 minutes at room temperature. Then top with the cream frosting and the remaining chopped walnuts. Slice away!

raw treats

raw cake

# Raspberry Cream Cacao Stacks

Like an Oreo, only more chic and raw. We love to make these stacked cookies when raspberries are in season: Raspberries are so irresistibly flavorsome when coupled with chocolate. These treats are the perfect sidekick to your afternoon cup of green tea.

## For the cookies
1 cup almonds
½ cup pecans
1 cup soft pitted dates
¼ cup cacao powder
2 tablespoons coconut sugar
1 teaspoon vanilla powder
2 pinches of salt

## For the raspberry cream
1 cup raspberries
3 tablespoons coconut butter
2 tablespoons rice malt syrup

**MAKES 8–10 STACKS**

First make the cookies. Place the almonds and pecans in a high-powered food processor and blend on high until fine, then add all the remaining ingredients and blend on high until well mixed. If the mixture isn't sticking together well (your dates may not be soft enough), add a tiny splash of water. Transfer the mixture to a piece of parchment paper; roll out using a rolling pin or top with another piece of parchment and press flat with a book.

Using a 2-inch round cookie cutter, cut out 16–20 cookies, re-rolling the dough as necessary. Place the cookies on a platter in the fridge for 1–2 hours until firm.

Meanwhile, make the raspberry cream. Add all the ingredients to the clean food processor and blend together until smooth. Transfer to a bowl and place in the fridge for 1 hour or until the cream has hardened slightly.

To assemble the stacks, take one cookie, dollop a large tablespoon of raspberry cream onto one side and place another cookie on top; return to the platter. Repeat. Place in the fridge for 30 minutes more to help the cream set slightly. Enjoy straight from the fridge!

93

94

raw cake

# Salted Caramel Crunch Bars

We've yet to meet anyone who can resist the temptation of these triple-layer bars, so keep them under lock and key! With biscuit, caramel and chocolate, they're everyone's favorites rolled into one.

## For the biscuit base

1 cup almonds

¼ cup raw whole buckwheat groats

1 cup pitted dates, soaked for 2 minutes (or use juicy Medjool dates)

¼ cup desiccated coconut

1 tablespoon tahini paste

3 generous pinches of Himalayan salt

## For the salted caramel layer

2 cups pitted dates, soaked until soft

3 tablespoons melted coconut oil

2 tablespoons tahini paste

2 tablespoons rice malt syrup or other liquid natural sweetener

3-5 pinches of salt, according to your taste

## For the crunch layer

½ cup almonds

¼ cup pumpkin seeds

¼ cup cacao nibs

2 tablespoons raw whole buckwheat groats

## For the drizzle topping

Raw Chocolate (see page 26)

MAKES 8—10 BARS

Line an 8-inch square baking pan with parchment paper.

First make the biscuit base. Place the almonds and buckwheat in a high-powered food processor and blend until chopped but not too fine. Then add all the remaining ingredients and blend until well combined. Press into the bottom of the baking pan.

For the salted caramel, blend the dates in the clean food processor on high. Add the coconut oil and tahini and blend again; to make sure you get this as smooth as possible, stop a few times and scrape down the sides with a spatula. Add salt to taste – we love to make this layer nice and salty. Smooth this over the biscuit base in the pan and place in the fridge while you prepare the next layer.

For the crunch layer, coarsely chop the almonds and pumkin seeds using a sharp knife. We don't use a blender so that we can keep this nice and chunky. Combine the almonds and pumpkin seeds with the cacao nibs and buckwheat in a large bowl. Press this dry mix into the salted caramel layer. Finish with a layer of Raw Chocolate – drizzle it over the top of the nuts from side to side.

Transfer to the fridge for 1 hour until firm; then cut into 8–10 bars. They will keep well in the fridge for up to 1 week.

95

# Rocky Road

This is one of our oldest recipes. When we first made it we couldn't believe how good it was and how quick it was to create. It might be fair to say that this recipe gave us faith that there was a whole world of raw desserts out there just waiting to be discovered. These bites are simultaneously soft, crunchy and seriously moreish.

### For the dry mixture
1 cup dried apricots (sulphur free)
½ cup walnuts
½ cup hazelnuts
½ cup currants or raisins (or a mix of both)
½ cup goji berries

### For the chocolate mixture
¾ cup melted coconut oil
¾ cup cacao powder
¼ cup coconut sugar
½ cup rice malt syrup
½ cup pitted dates, soaked for 30 minutes

MAKES 9–12 PIECES

Line a 6- or 8-inch square baking pan with parchment paper.

First make the dry mixture. Place all the ingredients in a high-powered food processor and pulse on high until just broken up and mixed together but still chunky. Transfer to a large mixing bowl.

Next make the chocolate mixture. Add the coconut oil, cacao, coconut sugar and rice malt syrup to the clean food processor and blend on high. Then add the dates and blend until smooth and combined. Make sure you don't overmix the chocolate or it can separate. If this happens and there is a lot of extra oil, add in some more cacao powder and malt syrup until it becomes smooth.

Pour the chocolate mixture over the dry mixture in the bowl and stir together with a large spoon until well combined. Scoop into the baking pan, pressing the mixture down to ensure it is compact (form a 6-inch square if using an 8-inch pan). Place in the fridge for 3–4 hours or the freezer for 1 hour, until the mixture is quite firm. Then cut into 9–12 pieces. They will keep well in the fridge for up to 7 days.

raw treats

# Oatmeal & Raisin Cookies

Sometimes there's really no point in reinventing the wheel. We've loved this simple, squidgy classic forever and this no-frills raw version is every bit as robust as the original. An absolute favorite of ours – dunk these cookies into tea or almond milk for best results!

1 cup rolled oats
½ cup pitted dates
½ cup coconut sugar
½ cup raisins, plus more
   for decorating
¼ cup rice malt syrup or other
   liquid natural sweetener
1 tablespoon melted coconut oil
1 teaspoon ground cinnamon
½ teaspoon vanilla powder

**MAKES 8 COOKIES**

Preheat the oven to no higher than 110°F or to its nearest low temperature, and line a baking sheet with parchment paper.

Place the oats and dates in a high-powered food processor and blend on high until fine. Add all the remaining ingredients and blend briefly, just until everything is well combined – you don't want the raisins to become too fine.

Separate the mixture into 8 equal balls, using your hands, and press each down into a flattened cookie shape on the parchment paper. Decorate the top of each cookie by pressing on a few raisins.

Place the cookies in the oven for 3–4 hours to dehydrate. They will keep well in the fridge for up to 1 week.

98

raw treats

# Fate
# Cookies

Fig + date = fate. Perfect partners in crime, these two have conspired to keep you going back to the cookie jar. You can't escape your fate.

1 cup dried figs

½ cup pitted dates

½ cup pecans

½ cup almonds

3 tablespoons melted coconut oil

2 tablespoons rice malt syrup or other liquid natural sweetener

2 tablespoons hulled sunflower seeds (optional)

2 tablespoons maca powder (optional)

½ tablespoon vanilla powder

pinch of salt

**MAKES 10–12 COOKIES**

Preheat the oven to no higher than 110°F or to its nearest low temperature, and line a baking sheet with parchment paper.

Place the figs, dates, pecans and almonds in a high-powered food processor and blend on high until mixed and quite fine. Add all the remaining ingredients and blend again until well combined.

Separate the mixture into 10–12 equal balls, using your hands, and press each ball down into a flattened cookie shape on the parchment paper.

Place the cookies in the oven for 3–4 hours to dehydrate. They will keep well in the fridge for up to 1 week.

# Dark Chocolate Truffles

½ cup rice malt syrup
½ cup cacao powder, plus
   more for a coating
¼ cup melted coconut oil
3 tablespoons cacao butter,
   melted
3 tablespoons coconut cream
finely chopped hazelnuts, for
   a coating

Luxuriously rich, these are next-level gooey and melt in your mouth like their traditional counterparts. Make a batch and box them up – they make great gifts for every occasion.

**MAKES 10–12 TRUFFLES**

Place all the ingredients except the hazelnuts in a high-powered food processor and blend on high. Then dollop the mixture into a bowl, cover and leave to set in the fridge for 2–3 hours – make sure it doesn't set completely hard, though, as it needs to be soft enough to scoop.

Use a teaspoon to scoop the chocolate into 10–12 balls (we roll them between glove-covered palms for ease).

Roll the balls in some cacao powder or finely chopped hazelnuts. Then transfer to a food storage container and chill in the fridge until needed. They will keep well in the fridge for up to 1 week.

101

# Jon Snow Balls

These luminous, dusted delights are a subtle nod to everyone's favorite *Game of Thrones* hero. Winter is coming.

½ cup cashews
½ cup desiccated coconut,
    plus more for a coating
2 tablespoons rice malt syrup
½ teaspoon vanilla powder
generous pinch of salt
coconut oil, for greasing

**MAKES 16 BALLS**

Place the cashews and desiccated coconut in a high-powered food processor and blend on high until as fine as possible. Add the rice malt syrup, vanilla powder and salt to the processor and blend again. If the mixture isn't sticky enough to hold together, blend in a dash of water.

Roll the mixture into 16 balls using the palms of your hands and then coat your palms with coconut oil before rolling each ball in some desiccated coconut. Transfer to a platter and chill in the fridge to set. The balls will keep in the fridge for 1 week.

raw treats

# Ginger & Apricot Bars

These bars are great. You can fix them up on a Sunday and keep going back for more throughout the week. We love the mellow taste of dried apricots offset by the spiciness of the fresh ginger.

½ cup dried apricots (we prefer sulphur free)

½ cup desiccated coconut

½ cup cashews

½ cup macadamia nuts

3 tablespoons rice malt syrup or other liquid natural sweetener

3 tablespoons grated fresh ginger root, plus more to taste

dried coconut flakes, for a topping

**MAKES 6–8 BARS**

---

Line a 6- or 8-inch square baking pan with parchment paper.

Place all the ingredients except the coconut flakes in a high-powered food processor and blend on high until as smooth as possible. Taste, then add more grated ginger if you like.

Transfer the mixture to the baking pan and press down evenly (form a 6-inch square if using an 8-inch pan). Press some coconut flakes on top of the mixture and transfer the pan to the freezer for 1 hour until firm.

Once firm, cut into 6–8 bars and enjoy. The bars will keep in the fridge for up to 5 days.

# Cold Brew Chocolate Cake

Who doesn't go weak at the knees at the thought of chocolate and coffee together? This gorgeously glutinous nutritional melting pot is our take on a rich, raw sponge cake.

## For the cake

4 cups pitted dates

4 cups cashews

5 tablespoons strong cold-brew coffee (see page 183)

½ cup cacao powder, more as needed

⅓ cup melted coconut oil

1 teaspoon vanilla powder

1 teaspoon salt

chopped cashews or cacao nibs, for sprinkling

## For the coffee frosting

2 cups cashews, soaked for 2 hours, rinsed and drained

1 cup strong cold-brew coffee

½ cup rice malt syrup or maple syrup

½ cup melted coconut oil

one 14-ounce (400 ml) can full-fat coconut milk, refrigerated overnight; use the top layer of cream only

*TIP:* If the coffee flavor needs a boost, whiz 1 tablespoon beans or organic coffee granules in a blender and add to the mix.

SERVES 6—8

Line a 6- or 8-inch square baking pan with parchment paper.

To make the cake, place the dates in a high-powered food processor and blend on high until they become a paste – you may need to stop the machine and scrape down the sides a few times until the mixture is nice and smooth. Set aside in a bowl.

Place the cashews in the clean food processor and blend until fine; add the coffee and cacao powder and blend until as smooth as possible. Add the coconut oil, vanilla, salt and date paste and blend until nicely combined. If there is too much oil, add some more cacao powder. Press half the mixture into the baking pan (form a 6-inch square if using an 8-inch pan) and place in the fridge to firm. Set the rest of the mixture aside.

To make the coffee frosting, blend the cashews with the coffee in the clean food processor on high until smooth. Blend in the remaining ingredients, adding the cream from the coconut milk last. Transfer the frosting to a bowl and place in the fridge for 2–3 hours until it stiffens up.

Spread half the frosting on top of the cake in the pan; return the frosted cake to the fridge for 30 minutes or until very firm. Then press the rest of the cake mixture over the frosted layer and refrigerate for 30 minutes more, until very firm.

Once firm, transfer the cake to a platter and spread with the remaining frosting. Transfer to the fridge for 1–2 hours until the frosting is firm enough for you to cut the cake (ideally leave overnight, if you can wait!). Sprinkle with chopped cashews or cacao nibs to decorate.

105

**raw treats**

raw cake

# Hazelnut & Chocolate Cupcakes

This has to be one of our absolute favorite recipes and even though our cupcake days are firmly behind us, there's still something to be said for a sweet that's equal parts cake and frosting.

## For the cake

1 cup pitted dates
1 cup hazelnuts, plus more, finely chopped, for sprinkling
1 cup almonds
½ cup raw whole buckwheat groats
½ cup coconut sugar
½ cup cacao powder
¼ cup cacao nibs
1 teaspoon grated nutmeg
generous pinch of Himalayan salt
4–5 tablespoons water

## For the hazelnut cream

1½ cups hazelnuts, soaked for 3 hours, rinsed and drained
¾ cup coconut cream (use the boxed variety or refrigerate a can of full-fat coconut milk overnight and then scoop off the cream that forms on top)
½ cup rice malt syrup or other liquid natural sweetener
½ cup melted coconut oil
½ cup pitted dates, soaked until soft
¼ cup almond milk, more as needed
¼ cup cacao powder, more as needed
1 teaspoon vanilla powder

MAKES 10 CUPCAKES

Preheat the oven to no higher than 110°F or to its nearest low temperature.

First make the cake. Place the dates hazelnuts, almonds and buckwheat in a high-powered food processor and blend on high until fine, then add all the remaining ingredients except the water and blend again. Add the water, 1 tablespoon at a time, until the mixture sticks together well but isn't wet.

Divide the cake mixture into 10 muffin or cupcake molds, pressing it onto the bottoms and up the sides but leaving the centers hollow to hold the cream topping. Place the molds on a baking sheet and dehydrate in the oven for 2 hours or until the cake has dried out nicely.

Meanwhile, make the cream. Blend the hazelnuts in the clean food processor until they are smooth. Add the remaining ingredients and blend until the mixture is creamy – this should take 5–10 minutes depending on your machine. The cream should be a soft, stiff texture, not too runny or hard. If it's too runny, add some more cacao, and if too hard a splash of almond milk should do the trick. If your food processor doesn't get the mixture smooth enough, transfer it to a high-speed blender like a Vitamix to get the perfect lump-free consistency. Pour the cream into a piping bag fitted with a wide tip.

Pipe the cream into each hollow cake, sprinkle with a few finely chopped hazelnuts and leave to set in the fridge overnight. Pop the cupcakes out of the molds carefully once the cream has set. They will keep in the fridge for 5 days.

107

# Nut-free Double Chocolate Brownies

A nut-free version of one of our first ever recipes, these chocolate brownies are every bit as indulgent as their nutty friend. In fact, we actually find the cacao to be more potent in this recipe than any of our others. Add in the benefits of the chia seeds and you've got yourself a powerhouse of energy and yumminess. Ideal for friends with nut allergies or anyone who fancies a change from nuts.

### For the brownies
½ cup pumpkin seeds
½ cup hulled sunflower seeds
½ cup coconut sugar
¼ cup chia seeds
¼ cup cacao nibs
1 tablespoon maca powder
1 tablespoon rice malt syrup
1½ cups pitted dates, soaked
½ cup cacao powder

### For the frosting
½ cup pitted dates, soaked
¼ cup cacao powder
¼ cup coconut sugar
¼ cup rice malt syrup or
    maple syrup
2 tablespoons coconut oil,
    melted

**MAKES 10–12 BROWNIES**

Line a 6- or 8-inch square baking pan with parchment paper.

Blend all the brownie ingredients except the dates and cacao powder in a high-powered food processor on high for 2–3 minutes until they are as fine as possible. Add the dates and cacao powder and blend until the mixture is nice and gooey and totally combined. Press into the baking pan (form a 6-inch square if using an 8-inch pan).

For the frosting, blend the dates in the clean food processor on high until nice and smooth. Add the remaining ingredients and blend until the mixture is gooey and creamy.

Spread the frosting on top of the brownie mixture, creating texture in the top with your spoon. Set in the fridge until the frosting is firm, for about 3 hours or ideally overnight. Cut into 10–12 squares. They will keep well in the fridge for up to 1 week.

# Raw Fig Rolls

An Egyptian classic made here on the streets of Shoreditch, London. Who'd have guessed it? These fig rolls are absolute party starters. Do the big reveal during an afternoon catch-up with friends.

## For the dough
¾ cup pitted dates
½ cup gluten-free rolled oats
½ cup desiccated coconut
¼ cup orange juice
½ teaspoon ground cinnamon
pinch of salt

## For the fig paste
1 cup dried figs, soaked for
   1 hour
½ cup pitted dates
zest of 1 orange

**MAKES 6–8 ROLLS**

Preheat the oven to no higher than 110°F or to its nearest low temperature. Line a baking sheet with parchment paper.

First make the dough. Blend the dates, oats and coconut in a high-powered food processor on high until fine, then add the orange juice, cinnamon and salt and blend until the mixture is soft and combined. Roll out the mixture into a rectangle approximately 6 by 8 inches on the baking sheet and place in the oven for 2 hours or until the top is dried out.

Meanwhile, make the fig paste. Remove the stalks from the soaked figs and add the figs, dates, and orange zest to the clean food processor. Mix until combined and gooey – you might have to stop the mixer a couple of times and scrape down the sides. Set aside in a bowl until the dough is ready.

Remove the dough from the oven and place a sheet of parchment paper and a cold baking sheet over the top. Hold the layers together and invert them; then remove the baking sheet and paper that are now on top – the exposed side of the dough should be slightly damper than the side that had been on top while drying.

Spread fig paste evenly in a strip lengthwise along the middle of the dough. Then carefully lift the paper on each long edge to fold the dough to the middle, over the filling. Transfer to the fridge to set for 30 minutes, then cut into 6–8 rolls. The rolls will keep well in the fridge for up to 1 week.

# Tiramisu

So many of our friends wanted us to recreate a raw version of this classic. There are many versions of this traditional Italian dessert, but the ladyfingers and the rich coffee flavor are paramount. Our portions are square, freestanding and dangerously delicious.

### For the base
1 cup walnuts
1 cup almonds
1 cup pitted dates, soaked
   until soft
¼ cup cacao powder
¼ cup almond milk
¼ cup coconut sugar

### For the ladyfinger logs
1 cup gluten-free rolled oats
1 cup pitted dates, soaked
   until soft
2 tablespoons cold-brew coffee
   (see page 183)
1 tablespoon maca powder
1 teaspoon vanilla powder

### For the cream
2 cups cashews
½ cup rice malt syrup or other
   liquid natural sweetener
¼ cup melted coconut oil
1 teaspoon vanilla powder
1 teaspoon lucuma powder
¼–½ cup filtered water

### For the topping
2 tablespoons coffee beans, plus
   more for decorating
2 tablespoons cacao nibs
cacao powder

**MAKES 4–6 SQUARES**

---

Line a 6- or 8-inch square baking pan with parchment paper.

To make the base, grind the nuts in a high-powered food processor on high until they become a fine flour. Add all the remaining ingredients; blend until combined and the mixture forms a sticky ball. Press the mixture evenly into the baking pan (form a 6-inch square if using an 8-inch pan); set aside.

To make the ladyfingers, grind the oats to a flour in the clean food processor on high speed. Add the dates and blend until smooth. Blend in the remaining ingredients. Roll the mixture into 4–6 fat fingers; place them on a plate – pressing down the top of each. Place in the fridge for 1–2 hours until firm.

For the cream layer, blend all the ingredients in the clean food processor until the mixture is smooth, adding the water gradually. Smoothly spread a quarter of the cream on top of the nut mixture in the pan and let it set in the fridge or freezer for 30 minutes.

When the ladyfingers are firm, lay them on top of the cream layer in the pan, then pour the rest of the cream on top. Set the pan the fridge overnight. If the cream is still very soft the next day, place it in the freezer for 30 minutes before serving.

To serve, blend the coffee beans and cacao nibs in the food processor on high to create a semi-fine dust. Remove the tiramisu from the pan; cut with a sharp knife into 4–6 pieces and dust with cacao powder and a sprinkling of the ground coffee bean-cacao nib mixture; dot with whole coffee beans.

**raw cake**

raw treats

From the Freezer

Chapter 4

**It's impossible to go wrong** with these frozen treats. They're perfect for stockpiling and revisiting any time you get the urge. We stock our freezer with these the way Grandma used to fill the extra freezer in the garage; relentlessly. Refreshing, indulgent, light or rich, there's something in here for every moment of need and the best thing is that they're absolutely 100 percent mistake-proof. We've always been suckers for collecting ice pop molds – it takes us back to our youth. You can do the same or stick to the standard molds that you can buy from supermarkets – it's totally up to you.

# Sencha & Almond Milk Pops

These Japanese-inspired creamy dream pops are hydrating and uplifting all at once. If you're struggling to get your hands on sencha, then use any other green tea you can find – the stronger the brew, the better.

For the cream layer

1 cup homemade almond milk (see page 21; it's important to use homemade for its creaminess and higher almond content)

1 cup cashews, soaked, rinsed and drained

¼ cup rice malt syrup or other liquid natural sweetener

For the green tea layer

1 cup strong brewed Sencha green tea or matcha

1 tablespoon rice malt syrup or other liquid natural sweetener (optional)

MAKES 6–8 POPS

First make the cream layer. Put all the ingredients in a high-powered food processor and blend on high until smooth.

Pour the almond cream into ice pop molds until each mold is half full. Place into the freezer for 2 hours or until frozen.

If you prefer your tea sweet, add the rice malt syrup to it when brewing. Once the tea is cool and the cream layer is frozen, pour the tea into the molds, insert the ice pop sticks and return the molds to the freezer for 3 hours more or overnight. Alternatively, you can pour your mixtures in thinner layers, creating stripes.

The pops will keep in the freezer for 2 weeks. To get them out of the molds easily, place the bottoms of the molds under warm running water to loosen them.

# Strawberry & Schisandra Pops

Putting the "pop" in ice pop, there's something undeniably cutesy about these fruity strawberry sensations. The recipe is endlessly versatile, too. Try replacing the strawberries with other berries such as raspberries, blackberries or blueberries, or go tropical with mango or pineapple. *(Pictured on pages 112–113.)*

1 cup strawberries
one 14-ounce (400 ml) can
   coconut milk
1 tablespoon maple syrup
1 tablespoon schisandra powder
pinch of Himalayan salt
desiccated coconut, for
   sprinkling

**MAKES 6—8 POPS**

Place the strawberries in a high-powered food processor and blend on high until broken down and smooth, then add the coconut milk, maple syrup, schisandra powder and salt and blend again for 1 minute – the mixture might separate slightly, but this will just give the pops a cute speckled appearance.

Sprinkle the desiccated coconut into the bottom of each ice pop mold. Pour the strawberry mixture into the molds and insert the ice pop sticks. Place in the freezer overnight.

The pops will keep in the freezer for 2 weeks. To get them out of the molds easily, place the bottoms of the molds under warm running water to loosen them.

116

# Cacao Fudge Pops

These are perfect for the kids, but you're probably not going to want to share them. The ideal summer's day indulgence, these are commercial Fudgsicle's older, cooler, plant-based brother. *(Pictured on pages 112-113.)*

½ cup cashews, soaked (either overnight in cool water or 1 hour in hot water), rinsed and drained

½ cup pitted dates, soaked until soft and drained

one 14-ounce (400 ml) can coconut milk

½ cup cacao powder

2 tablespoons coconut oil, melted

1 tablespoon maca powder (optional)

½ teaspoon vanilla powder

cacao nibs and raw whole buckwheat groats, for sprinkling

**MAKES 6—8 POPS**

Place the cashews in a high-powered food processor and blend on high until as fine as possible, then add the dates and blend together. Add the coconut milk, cacao powder, coconut oil, maca powder if using and vanilla, blending until the mixture is creamy with no lumps. This should take only a couple of minutes.

Sprinkle a few of the cacao nibs and buckwheat groats into the bottom of each ice pop mold. Pour the fudge mixture into the molds and insert the ice pop sticks. Place in the freezer overnight.

The pops will keep In the freezer for 2 weeks. To get them out of the molds easily, place the bottoms of the molds under warm running water to loosen them.

117

# Tea Cucumber Detox Coolers

Daily detox soothers, these refreshing ice pops are ideal for hydration. With the uplifting qualities of tea and cooling cucumber, these will clear brain fog and combat skin irritation as well as aging.

1 medium cucumber, peeled and seeded

2 cups cold-brewed tea of your choice (we used lemongrass green tea)

zest and juice of 1 lemon

1 tablespoon rice malt syrup or other liquid natural sweetener (optional)

1 tablespoon collagen powder (optional)

**MAKES 6—8 POPS**

Place the cucumber in a high-powered food processor and pulse until coarsely chopped but still very chunky. Add the tea, lemon juice and zest, and the rice malt syrup and collagen powder if using, and pulse until well combined.

Pour the mixture into ice pop molds and insert the ice pop sticks. Place in the freezer overnight.

The pops will keep in the freezer for 2 weeks. To get them out of the molds easily, place the bottoms of the molds under warm running water to loosen them.

### Cold-brewed Teas
Try switching the flavor of cold-brewed tea: camomile, honeysuckle flower, nettle, lemon verbena leaf and peppermint all work beautifully.

from the freezer

# Mint Chocolate Ice Pops

One for the boys, this creamy peppermint flavor is ideal for a midweek after-dinner clean treat. We find the hydrating qualities of spirulina so refreshing in this recipe, and with the addition of the emotionally uplifting, heart-opening qualities of raw cacao it's an all-round body and energy booster. You can find fresh mint in most supermarkets, but if you have the chance to use mint you've grown yourself you'll be blown away.

1 cup cashews, soaked for
   1 hour, rinsed and drained
¾ cup almond milk or other
   nut milk
¼ cup rice malt syrup
leaves from 2 fresh mint sprigs
¾ teaspoon spirulina powder
8-10 drops food-grade
   peppermint essential oil
1-2 tablespoons cacao nibs
Raw Chocolate (see page 26),
   for dipping

**MAKES 6—8 POPS**

Place the cashews and almond milk in a high-powered food processor and blend on high until smooth. Add the rice malt syrup, mint leaves, spirulina and peppermint oil and blend on high again until the mint is completely broken down. Stir in the cacao nibs to evenly distribute.

Pour the mixture into ice pop molds and insert the ice pop sticks. Place in the freezer overnight.

Remove the ice pops from their molds – run a little warm water on the bottoms of the molds if they are hard to get out. To finish, dip each pop in Raw Chocolate and place on a sheet of parchment paper set on a baking pan that will fit in your freezer. Once all the pops are dipped, return them to the freezer for 5–10 minutes to let the chocolate to set.

120

raw cake

# Purple Cream

We're a huge fan of açai bowls. We actually fell in love with them in Copenhagen, so when we created this recipe we wanted something similar but frozen, which could be served with an evening meal as a pudding and not just for breakfast.

2 cups frozen blueberries

1 cup cashews, soaked for 2 hours until soft, rinsed and drained

one 14-ounce (400 ml) can coconut milk, refrigerated overnight; use the top layer of cream only

¼ cup maple syrup or coconut syrup

¼ cup coconut sugar

1 tablespoon açai powder

¼ teaspoon vanilla powder or seeds of 1 vanilla pod

pinch of Himalayan salt

SERVES 2—4

Place all the ingredients in a high-powered food processor (scoop the layer of cream on top of the watery coconut milk into the processor) and blend on high until smooth. Pour the mixture into a freezerproof container (or ice pop molds), cover, and freeze for 2–3 hours or overnight.

Once the mixture is scoopable, scoop and serve. If it is hard, blend it again in the food processor before serving.

123

# Cookie Dough Ice Cream

We admit the inspiration: everyone's favorite Ben & Jerry's flavor. You'll watch the whole bowl of this naturally, creamy nuttiness disappear as you hunker down for a Saturday night on the sofa with this beauty. Every bit as delicious as the original, this is Nature's way of showing how much it loves you.

## For the ice cream

⅞ cup coconut milk (half a 14-ounce/400 ml can), refrigerated overnight; use the top layer of cream only

½ cup homemade almond milk (see page 21; it's important to use homemade for its creaminess and higher almond content)

½ cup cashews, soaked, rinsed and drained

¼ cup coconut sugar

½ teaspoon vanilla powder

pinch of salt

## For the cookie dough pieces

½ cup cashews

½ cup pitted Medjool dates

¼ cup coconut sugar

¼ teaspoon vanilla powder

pinch of Himalayan salt

**SERVES 2**

First make the ice cream. Scoop out the layer of cream on the top of the watery coconut milk, and place it in a high-speed food processor. Add all the remaining ingredients, and then blend on high until smooth. Transfer to a medium freezerproof container, cover and freeze for 2–3 hours until the mixture is solid.

Meanwhile make the cookie dough pieces. Blend all the ingredients together in the clean food processor. Scrape the sides down a couple of times and re-blend until the mixture is gooey and fine. Spread the mixture in a thin layer on a baking sheet and place in the fridge for 1–2 hours until chilled and less sticky. Then roll it into small uneven balls using your hands.

When ready to serve, remove the ice cream from the freezer. Break up the block and put the pieces back into the clean food processor; pulse until they blend into a creamy texture, taking care not to overmix here. Serve immediately, dotting the cookie dough balls onto the ice cream.

124

from the freezer

# Sea
# Green
# Sorbet

Sea green sorbet is basically edible algae and vegetables masquerading deliciously as a sweet. The addition of hydrating apple and kiwi boosts its vitamin C content and gives the sorbet a tantalizingly tart flavor. It's also surprisingly great to eat before bed, thanks to the magnesium in spinach. The kids will never know.

2 handfuls of fresh spinach
    (about 2 cups)
flesh of 1 avocado, cubed and
    frozen
2 apples, cored and quartered
2 kiwis, skinned and quartered
1 lime, peeled
½ tablespoon spirulina powder
½ tablespoon chlorella powder
½ tablespoon wheatgrass
    powder

**SERVES 2–4**

Place the spinach, avocados, apples, kiwis and lime in a high-powered food processor and blend on high for 3–5 minutes until smooth. Add the powders (if you don't have them all, add the ones you have or perhaps a green powder blend) and blend until as smooth as possible.

Transfer to a freezerproof container or ice cube trays, cover, and freeze for 4–6 hours.

When ready to serve, remove the sorbet from the freezer. Break up the block and put the pieces back into the clean food processor. Re-blend the frozen mixture briefly; when it becomes an icy sorbet texture, stop blending and serve straight away.

*Kiwi*
A great source of vitamin C, tangy, succulent kiwis also contain a protein-dissolving enzyme that can help with digestion after a large meal.

# Cinnamon Coffee Cream

A deviously delicious blend of two grown-up flavors: The uplifting aroma of coffee and the grounding homeyness of cinnamon are a harmonious duo. There's nothing Bridget Jones about eating an entire bowl of this.

1 cup strong cold-brew coffee (see page 183)

½ cup cashews, soaked, rinsed and drained, plus more if needed

½ cup almond milk or other non-dairy milk

2 tablespoons maple syrup

¼ teaspoon ground cinnamon

**SERVES 2**

Place all the ingredients in a high-powered food processor and blend on high until the mixture becomes creamy. If it looks too watery, add some more cashews to thicken it up.

Transfer to a freezerproof container or ice cube trays, cover, and freeze for 4–5 hours.

When ready to serve, remove the cream from the freezer. Break up the block and put the pieces back into the clean food processor. Re-blend the frozen mixture briefly; when it becomes an icy sorbet texture, stop blending and serve straight away.

# Lemon, Mango & Ginger Ginseng Sorbet

Zesty and uplifting, with the delicate sweetness of mango and a little ginger kick, we sometimes can't believe that this sorbet is nutritious as well as delicious. With the detoxifying qualities of lemon and the anti-inflammatory qualities of ginger, you'll certainly have a spring in your step after eating this.

1 large mango, peeled and pitted

zest and juice of 1 lemon

¼ cup filtered water

3 tablespoons rice malt syrup or other liquid natural sweetener

2-inch piece of fresh ginger root, peeled

1 teaspoon Siberian ginseng (optional)

desiccated or flaked coconut, for a garnish

**SERVES 2—4**

Place all the ingredients except the coconut in a high-powered food processor and blend on high until smooth. Pour into a medium freezerproof container or ice-cube trays, cover, and freeze for 3–4 hours until fully frozen.

When ready to serve, remove the sorbet from the freezer. Break up the block and put the pieces back into the clean food processor. Re-blend the frozen mixture briefly; when it becomes an icy sorbet texture, stop blending and serve straight away, garnished with the coconut.

from the freezer

raw cake

# Cherry, Lucuma & Banana Ice Cream

In this recipe, banana ice cream gets a cheeky cherry twist. It's best to make this using cherries only when they are in season, otherwise you'll find that the fruit won't be as tasty and the sweet cherry flavor won't come through. If cherries are not in season, you can easily create this recipe with many other fruits, including blueberries, strawberries, raspberries or figs. Try experimenting with your favorites.

1½ cups halved and pitted fresh sweet cherries
1 tablespoon coconut syrup
2½ bananas, sliced and frozen
1 tablespoon lucuma powder

**SERVES 2**

Place one-third of the cherries and the coconut syrup in a high-powered food processor and pulse until coarse. Set aside in a bowl or cup.

Place the bananas in the food processor. Add half of the remaining cherries and the lucuma powder and blend for 3–4 minutes on high. The blender might struggle for the first 30 seconds, but then the bananas will break into pieces and eventually will become smooth. Blend until everything is smooth, but don't overmix or the bananas will start to melt. (This should take 2–3 minutes depending on your machine.)

Layer the blended cherries, banana ice cream and the remaining fresh cherries into glasses or bowls and serve straight away.

131

Chapter 5

**Cheesecakes are the crowning glory** of raw desserts and the holy grail for those who make them. They are what we're most known for and they took us an age to master. If we had a penny for every cheesecake we had to pour into a glass and serve as a mousse, we'd be rich. It took experience for us to recognize when they were perfectly mixed, and practice to make them neatly and master our decoration style. These beauties are tricky but once you get there the showstoppingly impressive results will be more than worth the learning curve. Of course, there is always the chance you'll get it the first time: You won't know until you try!

# White Chocolate Raspberry Cheesecake

A real centerpiece, this cheesecake will be the star of the show at any dinner party. We love that the fresh raspberries peek through the cake and its luxurious beet base. For a different, herby, botanical look, sprinkle fresh amaranth on top. Present this cake with pride, it's a beauty. *(Pictured on pages 132–133.)*

**For the base**
1 cup cashews
1 cup desiccated coconut
3 tablespoons rice malt syrup
2 tablespoons beet powder
   (or use beet juice if you
   don't have powder)
pinch of Himalayan salt

**For the filling**
2 cups cashews, soaked for
   1-2 hours, rinsed and
   drained
1 cup diced fresh coconut
   meat
1 cup rice malt syrup
½ cup coconut oil
¼ cup almond milk
3 tablespoons lemon juice
2 tablespoons cacao butter
1 teaspoon vanilla powder
½ pint fresh raspberries
cashew cream (see page 80),
   for decorating
edible flowers, for decorating

**SERVES 12—16**

Line an 8-inch round springform cake pan with parchment paper.

For the base, place the cashews and coconut in a high-powered food processor and blend on high until fine. Then add the rice malt syrup, beet powder and salt and blend again until well combined. Press the base into the bottom of the springform pan.

For the filling, add the cashews to the clean food processor or a high-speed blender (for extra smoothness) and blend on high until well broken up. Add the coconut meat and blend again, making sure it combines with the cashews. Then add the rice malt syrup, coconut oil, almond milk, lemon juice, cacao butter and vanilla and blend for 2 minutes more until the mixture has a smooth, creamy consistency.

Arrange all but a few of the raspberries on top of the base in the pan and pour the filling mixture over them, making sure they're covered. Place the pan in the fridge overnight or in the freezer for 2–3 hours to set. The cake will keep well (undecorated) in the fridge for up to 3 days.

When ready to serve, remove the cake from the springform pan. Pipe some cashew cream in a pretty pattern along the top edge and decorate with the remaining raspberries and some edible flowers.

135

# Nut-free Coconut & Lime Mousse Cake

Most raw cheesecakes rely on nuts, but this light and airy variation doesn't need them. Fresh and uplifting, the tart lime works in harmony with the soothing creamy coconut to create a delicate yet decadent dessert. Serve this cut into cubes in our signature style and you're looking at a winner.

### For the base

1 cup desiccated coconut
¼ cup gluten-free rolled oats
¼ cup raw whole buckwheat groats
1 tablespoon golden flax seeds
1 tablespoon tulsi (optional)
zest of 1 lime
generous pinch of salt
3 tablespoons rice malt syrup

### For the filling

1 cup desiccated coconut
1¾ cups (400 ml) canned coconut cream
¾ cup rice malt syrup
½ cup coconut oil
3 tablespoons lime juice
1 tablespoon cacao butter
zest of half a lime
pinch of Himalayan salt

### For decorating

thin slices of fresh lime
desiccated coconut
bee pollen (see note on safe use, page 181)

**SERVES 6–8**

Line a 6- or 8-inch square baking pan with parchment paper. (If using an 8-inch pan, first use aluminum foil to block off a 2-inch section along one edge.)

For the base, place all the ingredients except the rice malt syrup in a high-powered food processor and pulse until coarsely broken up. Add the rice malt syrup and blend until medium-fine and well combined. Press into the bottom of the baking pan.

For the filling, place the desiccated coconut in the clean food processor and blend until fine like flour. Add all the remaining filling ingredients and pulse until everything is well combined and smooth, making sure the desiccated coconut has combined well. Pour the mixture, which should be quite runny, over the base in the pan and quickly transfer the pan to the freezer; let freeze for 2–3 hours until well set.

If the cake is rock solid when you take it out, let it thaw for 20–30 minutes before serving. It will keep in the fridge for up to 3 days.

To serve, cut the cake into cubes and decorate with lime slices, desiccated coconut and bee pollen.

136

raw cheesecakes

# Ginger Chai Latte Cheesecake

For this recipe we wanted to use some of our favorite, more sophisticated flavors. Warming ginger, cardamom, cinnamon, nutmeg and allspice make this cheesecake a feast for the soul. If chai lattes are your go-to beverage, this dessert is the one for you.

### For the base
1 cup cashews
½ cup walnuts
2" peeled fresh ginger, chopped
½ cup coconut sugar
1 cup pitted dates

### For the filling
2½ cups cashews, soaked until soft, rinsed and drained
1 cup melted coconut oil
1 cup rice syrup
2" peeled fresh ginger, chopped
seeds from 10-14 cardamom pods
½ teaspoon each ground cinnamon, allspice, nutmeg
¼ teaspoon vanilla powder
pinch of ground black pepper

### For the crumble topping
½ cup cashews
½ cup walnuts
½ teaspoon ground cinnamon
seeds from 6 cardamom pods
pinch of ground black pepper

### For the toffee drizzle
½ cup pitted dates, soaked
½ cup maple syrup
1 tablespoon tahini paste
1 tablespoon maca powder
¼ teaspoon vanilla powder
pinch of Himalayan salt

SERVES 8–12

Line an 8-inch round cake pan or pie dish with parchment paper.

To make the base, place the nuts in a high-powered blender and blend coarsely, then add the ginger, coconut sugar and dates and blend until well combined. Press into the cake pan.

For the filling, blend the cashews in a high-powered food processor until they are as smooth as possible, add the remaining ingredients and blend on high until everything has broken down and become smooth. Pour the filling over the base in the cake pan.

For the crumble topping, add all the ingredients to the clean food processor and pulse slowly so that everything combines but still remains very coarse. Pour this on top of the filling and press down gently. Place the pan in the fridge overnight or in the freezer for 2–4 hours to set.

Meanwhile, make the toffee drizzle. Drain the dates and place them in the clean food processor. Blend on high until broken up, then add all the other ingredients and blend again until smooth. If the mixture is quite thick, add 1–2 tablespoons of warm water so that it will drizzle easily.

When you're ready to eat, remove the cheesecake from the fridge or freezer, drizzle the toffee sauce on top and serve.

138

# Macadamia Cinnamon Cheesecake

Macadamia nuts are a great addition to cashews when making raw cheesecakes. They are well worth their high price tag because of their creamy texture and flavor. The sophisticated flavors in this cheesecake were inspired by figs we foraged in Ibiza.

## For the base
2½ cups dried figs
1 cup almonds
2 tablespoons rice malt syrup
1 tablespoon maca powder
    (optional)
pinch of salt
¼ cup cacao powder
2 tablespoons coconut sugar

## For the filling
1½ cups cashews,
    soaked for 2 hours in cold
    water or 30 minutes in warm
½ cup macadamia nuts,
    soaked as cashews
½ cup rice malt syrup
¼ cup coconut milk
¼ cup lemon juice
¼ cup coconut oil
2 tablespoons ground cinnamon,
    plus more to taste
1 tablespoon cacao butter,
    melted
dried coconut flakes, for
    decorating

SERVES 8—10

Soak 1 cup of the dried figs in water for 30 minutes. Meanwhile, line a 6- or 8-inch square baking pan with parchment paper. (If using an 8-inch pan, first use aluminum foil to block off a 2-inch section along one edge.)

To make the base, drain the soaked figs and place them in a high-powered food processor. Blend on high until broken up. Then add the almonds, rice malt syrup, maca powder if using and salt; blend again. Add the cacao powder and blend again just to combine. Press the mixture into the bottom of the baking pan.

Next add the remaining figs and the coconut sugar to the clean food processor and blend until coarse. Crumble this mixture over the base in the pan and set aside.

For the filling, rinse and drain the nuts and add to the clean food processor. Blend on high until as fine as possible. Then add the rest of the ingredients except the coconut flakes, blending until there are no lumps. Taste the filling and add more cinnamon if you like.

Pour the filling over the base in the pan, making sure it is all covered. Put the pan in the fridge overnight or the freezer for 2–3 hours until set. Decorate the cake with some coconut flakes before serving.

139

raw cake

# Toffee Cacao Cheesecake

This super-indulgent, velvety cheesecake with chocolate, brownie and toffee layers is guaranteed to fulfill the most insatiable of chocolate cravings. With maca, chaga, cacao nibs and cacao powder, it's a real slice of the nutritionally delicious.

## For the base
½ cup pecans
½ cup hazelnuts
1 cup pitted dates
¼ cup cacao nibs
1 tablespoon maca powder
1 tablespoon chaga powder
½ teaspoon salt
Nut-free Double Chocolate
    Brownies (see page 108)

## For the filling
2 cups cashews, soaked, rinsed
    and drained
½ cup coconut milk
1 cup Date Paste (see page 26)
½ cup coconut oil
½ cup almond butter
½ cup rice malt syrup
½ cup cacao powder
1 tablespoon maca powder
1 teaspoon vanilla powder
½ teaspoon salt

## For decorating
Date Paste
chopped chocolate chunks

SERVES 8–12

Line a 9-inch round springform cake pan with parchment paper.

For the base, blend the pecans and hazelnuts in a high-powered food processor on high until ground. Add the dates, cacao nibs, maca powder, chaga powder and salt and blend until well combined and slightly gooey. Press the mixture into the bottom of the springform pan.

For the filling, add the cashews to the clean food processor and blitz for 1–2 minutes until very smooth. Add the coconut milk and pulse. Add the rest of the ingredients and mix until thick and smooth.

To assemble, break some of the brownies into small chunks and scatter them over the base in the springform pan. Pour the filling over the base and place the pan in the fridge for 3–4 hours or overnight to set.

When ready to serve, remove the cake from the springform pan. Place some date paste in a piping bag fitted with a wide tip and pipe decoratively around the top edge of the cake. Decorate with chopped chocolate chunks and serve with the remaining brownies.

# Hawaiian Cheesecake

An exotic twist on traditional cheesecake, this Hawaii-inspired dream will take you to the Pacific and back in a single mouthful. The goji berries in the base are a particularly special touch, and who can resist fresh pineapple?

## For the base
½ cup cashews
½ cup almonds
¼ cup goji berries
¼ cup rice malt syrup
1 tablespoon maca powder
pinch of salt
1 cup pitted dates, soaked if
 very hard

## For the cheesecake layers
3 cups cashews
1½ cups fresh diced pineapple
1¼ cups rice malt syrup or
 maple syrup
1 cup melted coconut oil
½ cup desiccated coconut
1 tablespoon vanilla powder

## For the pineapple sorbet
2 cups fresh diced pineapple,
 plus more for a topping
¼ cup rice malt syrup
½ cup melted coconut oil

**SERVES 8—12**

Line an 8-inch round springform cake pan with parchment paper.

For the base, place all the ingredients except the dates in a high-powered food processor and blend on high briefly to combine, then add the dates and blend again until well combined. Press the mixture into the bottom of the springform pan.

For the cheesecake layers, place the cashews in a high-powered blender and blend on high until they are very smooth. Add all the remaining ingredients and blend again on high for a few minutes until the mixture is smooth. Pour half this mixture on top of the base in the pan; place in the freezer to set. Set the rest of the mixture aside.

Meanwhile, make the pineapple sorbet. Blend the pineapple and rice malt syrup together in the clean blender; pour into a fine sieve and drain all the excess juice. Return the pineapple mixture to the blender, add the coconut oil and blend. Pour into a bowl and put in the fridge for 30 minutes. When the sorbet is slightly set, spoon it over the cheesecake layer in the pan, smooth down, then pour the rest of the cheesecake mixture over it.

Place the cake in the freezer for 2 hours or the fridge overnight to set. When ready to serve, remove the cake from the springform pan and decorate with the extra diced pineapple. Serve chilled.

# Cacao Mint Layer Cake

Adapted from one of our best-sellers, this triple-decker delight is the perfect dinner party serve. With cacao, spirulina and wheatgrass, it packs a serious superfood punch while the peppermint oil cuts refreshingly through the sweetness.

## For the base
½ cup almonds

½ cup walnuts

1½ cups desiccated coconut

1 cup pitted Medjool dates (if not Medjool, soak to soften)

¼ cup cacao powder

¼ cup rice malt syrup

¼ teaspoon Himalayan salt

## For the mint filling
1½ cups cashews, soaked for 2 hours, rinsed and drained

1½ cups melted coconut oil

2 tablespoons rice syrup

1 tablespoon spirulina powder

1 tablespoon wheatgrass powder

10-15 drops food-grade peppermint essential oil

## For the chocolate frosting
½ cup cashews, soaked for 2 hours, rinsed and drained

1 cup melted coconut oil

½ cup rice malt syrup

¼ cup cacao powder, plus more if needed

1 tablespoon cacao butter, melted

1 teaspoon vanilla powder

**SERVES 8—12**

Line an 8-inch round springform cake pan with parchment paper.

For the base, place the almonds and walnuts in a high-powered food processor and blitz until coarsely ground. Then add the remaining ingredients and blend on high until well combined. Press the mixture into the bottom of the springform pan.

For the mint filling, blend the cashews in the clean food processor on high until as smooth as possible. Add the remaining ingredients and blend again on high. Pour this mixture over the base in the pan and place in the freezer for 20-30 minutes until firm.

Meanwhile, for the frosting, blend the cashews in the clean food processor on high until as smooth as possible. Then add the remaining ingredients, blitzing until smooth. If the mixture is too oily, add some extra cacao powder; if it's too rough and not shiny, add a small splash of water.

Pour the frosting over the firm mint layer in the pan and place in the fridge overnight or the freezer for 2-4 hours. When ready to serve, remove the cake from the springform pan. Serve chilled. It will keep well for up to 5 days in the fridge.

143

raw cake

# Chocolate Orange Rocky Road Cake

Adding pieces of our vegan Rocky Road to this flavorsome cake takes it to the next level, but if you prefer to keep things simple you can always leave them out.

## For the base

1 cup cashews

1 cup pecans

1 cup desiccated coconut

1 cup pitted Medjool dates (if not Medjool, soak to soften)

¼ cup cacao powder

1 tablespoon maca powder (optional)

pinch of salt

small chunks of Rocky Road (see page 96)

## For the filling

3 cups cashews, soaked for 2 hours, rinsed and drained

1½ cups melted coconut oil

¾ cup cacao powder, plus more if needed

1 cup rice malt syrup

1 cup freshly squeezed orange juice, plus more if needed

zest of 1 orange

pinch of Himalayan salt

## For decorating

dehydrated orange pieces, cacao nibs, and edible flowers or Dark Chocolate Truffles (see page 101)

Line an 8-inch round springform cake pan with parchment paper.

For the base, place the cashews, pecans and desiccated coconut in a high-powered food processor and blend on high until coarsely chopped. Add the remaining ingredients except the Rocky Road, and blend on high until well combined. Press the mixture into the bottom of the springform pan. Then crumble a few handfuls of the Rocky Road over the base.

For the filling, place the cashews in a high-powered blender or food processor and blend until they are broken down and fine. Add the remaining ingredients and blend for up to 5 minutes (depending on your machine) until the mixture is completely smooth. If it looks too runny, add some extra cacao powder; if it's too thick, add some more orange juice.

Pour the filling into the springform pan, over the Rocky Road pieces, and then place the pan in the fridge overnight or in the freezer for 3–4 hours to firm. Keep in the fridge until ready to serve.

When ready to serve, remove the cake from the springform pan. Decorate with dehydrated orange pieces, cacao nibs and edible flowers or Dark Chocolate Truffles. Serve chilled.

# Blueberry Lemon Swirl Cheesecake

Colored swirls are the *pièce de résistance* of the cheesecake world. We used to be in awe of them before we learned how to create them ourselves. Stick with it – if you don't get it right first time, you can refine your technique with each attempt! *(Pictured on pages 146-147.)*

**For the base**

1 cup cashews

½ cup pecans

½ cup soft pitted dates

2 tablespoons rice malt syrup or other liquid natural sweetener

1 tablespoon maca powder (optional)

pinch of Himalayan salt

**For the filling and topping**

¾ cup desiccated coconut

3 cups cashews, soaked in warm water for 2 hours and drained

1 cup rice malt syrup or other liquid natural sweetener, plus more if needed

1 cup melted coconut oil

½ cup lemon juice, plus more if needed

zest of 1 lemon, plus more for decorating

½ teaspoon turmeric powder

2 cups fresh or frozen blueberries

edible flowers and coconut flakes, for decorating

**SERVES 8—12**

For the base, line an 8-inch round springform cake pan with parchment paper. Place the nuts in a high-powered food processor and blend on high until coarsely ground. Then blend in the remaining ingredients until well mixed. Press the mixture into the bottom of the springform pan.

For the filling, place the coconut in a high-powered blender and blend on high until fine, then add the cashews, rice malt syrup and coconut oil and blend again until the mixture is as smooth as possible, scraping down the sides to incorporate everything. Transfer half the mixture to a bowl and set aside.

Add the lemon juice, zest and turmeric to the mixture left in the blender and blend until smooth. Taste, and add more lemon juice if it needs more flavor, and more syrup if it's too tart. Pour into a second bowl, transferring a few tablespoons of this lemon cream to a piping bag to chill for later. Return the other half of the mixture to the blender and add the blueberries. Blend until combined and add more syrup if needed. Pour this mixture back into the bowl.

Spoon equal dollops of the purple mixture and the yellow mixture at random onto the cake base, alternating between colors, until you have used both up. Wiggle the pan from side to side to settle the mixtures, and then swirl a knife through them to create a pattern. Place the pan in the fridge overnight or the freezer for 3–4 hours until firm. When ready to serve, remove the cake from the springform pan; pipe on the reserved lemon cream, and dot with edible flowers, coconut flakes and lemon zest. Serve chilled.

**raw cake**

# Peanut Butter Cheesecake

Don't let the simplicity of this recipe fool you. When you've made it once, you'll keep dreaming about it until you make it again. We first made this for a peanut butter-obsessed friend and now we make it at least once a month!

### For the base

¼ cup raw unsalted peanuts

¼ cup almonds

1 cup pitted Medjool dates (if not Medjool, soak to soften)

2 tablespoons golden flax seeds

½ tablespoon peanut butter

pinch of Himalayan salt

### For the filling

3 large or 4 small bananas

1 cup peanut butter

¼ cup rice malt syrup

¼ cup melted coconut oil

1 tablespoon maca powder

¼ teaspoon vanilla powder

SERVES 8–12

Line an 8-inch round springform cake pan with parchment paper.

For the base, place the peanuts and almonds in a high-powered food processor and blend on high for a few seconds to coarsely chop. Add the dates, flax seeds, peanut butter and salt and blend until the mixture is well combined and slightly sticky. Press the mixture into the base of the springform pan.

For the filling, put the bananas and peanut butter into the food processor and blend until combined. Add the rice malt syrup, coconut oil, maca powder and vanilla powder and blend until the mixture is smooth. Pour the filling into the springform pan over the base, and then put the pan in the fridge for 3–4 hours to firm.

When ready to serve, remove the cake from the springform pan. Enjoy!

149

**Chapter 4**

**As perfect sharers**, these are what we turn to when we're supposed to be sharing. If "hostess with the mostess" is the accolade you're aiming for, these are for you. We whip these up when we want people to believe we're grown-ups – and the trick works every time.

# Lemon Baobab Curd Pie

Our take on a lemon meringue pie, the baobab in this complements the zesty lemon flavors seamlessly. This is an absolute crowd pleaser and a centerpiece to any dinner party table. *(Pictured on pages 150–151.)*

## For the crust

1 cup desiccated coconut

½ cup cashews

3 tablespoons rice malt syrup

1 tablespoon tahini paste

1 tablespoon lucuma powder (optional)

zest of 1 lemon

## For the lemon filling

½ cup cashews, soaked for 1–2 hours, rinsed and drained

½ cup lemon juice

¼ cup coconut oil

one 14-ounce (400 ml) can coconut milk, refrigerated overnight; use the top layer of cream only

¼ cup rice malt syrup

3 tablespoons chia seeds, covered in water and soaked for 20 minutes

½ tablespoon baobab powder

1 teaspoon turmeric powder

zest of 1 lemon, plus more for a garnish

pinch of salt

## For the coconut cream whip

two 14-ounce (400 ml) cans coconut milk, refrigerated overnight; use the top layer of cream only

2 tablespoons rice malt syrup

**SERVES 8—12**

Line an 8-inch pie dish with parchment paper.

For the crust, place the coconut and cashews in a high-powered food processor and blend on high until coarsely chopped. Add the remaining ingredients along with 2 tablespoons of water and blend again until the mixture is fine and well combined. Press the crust mixture into the bottom and up the sides of the pie dish.

For the filling, place the cashews, lemon juice and coconut oil in a high-powered blender and blend on high until the cashews have broken down as much as possible. Scoop the layer of cream on the top of the coconut milk into the blender; add the remaining ingredients and blend again on high until the mixture is smooth and creamy. Pour the filling mixture into the crust in the pie dish. Put the pie in the fridge for 3–4 hours or overnight to set.

Finally, make the coconut cream whip. Scoop the layer of cream on the top of the coconut milk into the clean food processor; add the rice malt syrup and blend on high until the cream becomes smooth and lump-free. Don't overmix or the cream will become too sloppy.

Spoon the coconut cream whip over the lemon pie and return the pie to the fridge until ready to serve. Then garnish each slice with a scattering of lemon zest.

153

# Maple Maca Pecan Pie

Maple maca pecan pie – try saying that with your mouth full! We brought this straight from the States to London, with a superfood booster. Whichever side of the pond you're on, it won't stay in your fridge for long.

## For the crust
2 cups pecans
1 cup pitted dates, soaked for
   30 minutes to soften if hard
2 tablespoons tahini paste
2 tablespoons maca powder
generous pinch of salt

## For the filling
2 cups pecans, plus 24 pretty
   pecan halves for decorating
4 cups pitted dates, soaked for
   30 minutes to soften if hard
¾ cup melted coconut oil
½ cup almond milk
¼ cup maple syrup
2 tablespoons maca powder
½ teaspoon ground cinnamon
generous pinch of salt

**SERVES 8—12**

Line an 8-inch pie dish with parchment paper.

First make the crust. Place the pecans in a high-powered blender and blitz on high until they are coarsely chopped. Add all the remaining ingredients and blend until well combined. If the mixture doesn't stick together when pressed, add 1 tablespoon of water. Press the crust mixture into bottom and up the sides of the pie dish.

For the filling, blend the pecans in the blender or a food processor until they are as fine as possible. Add the dates and blend again. Throw in the remaining ingredients and blitz again on high until everything is well combined. Stop and scrape down the sides a few times to make sure the mixture is as smooth as possible.

Scoop the filling into the crust and flatten down using a spatula. Press the pecan halves into the top to decorate. Place in the fridge for at least 2 hours before cutting and serving.

154

tarts, pies & pudding pots

raw cake

# Salted Chocolate Chickpea Tart

This might sound a little unusual, but it was love at first bite for us. Chickpeas become smooth and gooey when blended and this protein-rich dessert is wonderfully dense, rich and sumptuous. No one will believe it's made of super-nutritious soaked chickpeas.

SERVES 8–12

### For the base
1 cup cashews

½ cup Brazil nuts

¼ cup coconut sugar

3 tablespoons raw cacao powder

seeds of half a vanilla pod or
   ½ teaspoon vanilla powder

pinch of Himalayan salt

1 cup pitted Medjool dates, (if
   not Medjool, soak to soften)

### For the filling
2 cups raw chickpeas, soaked for
   24 hours, rinsed and drained

½ cup rice malt syrup or maple
   syrup

½ cup pitted Medjool dates, (if
   not Medjool, soak to soften)

¼ cup coconut sugar

¼ cup raw cacao powder

2 tablespoons almond or other
   nut milk

seeds of 1½ vanilla pods, or
   1 teaspoon vanilla powder

¼ teaspoon Himalayan salt

fresh edible flower petals, for
   a garnish (optional)

Line an 8-inch round tart pan with parchment paper.

First, make the base. Place the cashews and Brazil nuts in a high-powered food processor and blend on high until they are as fine as possible. Add the coconut sugar, cacao powder, vanilla seeds and salt and blend again until they are combined. Then add the dates and keep blending until the mixture sticks together well. If it is too crumbly, then add 1 tablespoon of water to help bind it. Press the base mixture into the bottom of the tart pan.

For the filling, place all the ingredients except the flower petals in the clean food processor and blend on high for 5–8 minutes. Keep blending until the mixture becomes silky smooth and is not grainy any more. Pour the filling mixture onto the base in the tart pan, spreading it out evenly, and put in the fridge for 1–2 hours to set.

Serve the tart chilled. We like to finish this dessert by decorating it with fresh bachelor button petals for an extra flourish.

*NOTE*: If you can't get hold of raw (dried) chickpeas, then canned will work perfectly for this recipe, but do bear in mind that they have been cooked.

157

raw cake

# Banana Lucuma Pies

Lucuma's nutritional benefits plus its biscuity flavor make this banana pie everything you are imagining and more. Even pictures don't do it justice. Rich in magnesium and potassium from the bananas, this is grounding, relaxing and delicious.

## For the crust

1½ cups cashews, plus more, chopped, for sprinkling
1½ cups desiccated coconut
2 tablespoons lucuma powder
generous pinch of salt

## For the filling

3 large bananas
½ cup coconut milk
½ cup Date Paste (see page 26)
½ cup coconut oil
1 tablespoon lemon juice
2 tablespoons lucuma powder
½ teaspoon vanilla powder
2 pinches of salt

## For the caramel sauce

1 cup pitted dates, soaked for 10 minutes in warm water or 1 hour in cold to soften if hard
½ cup water
¼ cup almond butter
1 tablespoon rice malt syrup or other liquid natural sweetener
½ teaspoon vanilla powder
generous pinch of salt

**MAKES FOUR 3-INCH MINI PIES**

We use 3-inch mini fluted tart pans for these. If your pans don't have removable bottoms, line them with pieces of parchment paper that come up the sides.

For the crust, place the cashews in a high-powered blender and blend on high until chopped, then add the remaining ingredients and 1 tablespoon of water and mix until semi-fine (ideally you want a few chunks remaining). Press the crust mixture onto the bottom and up into the fluted sides of the mini pans. Put in the fridge while you make the filling.

Set aside half of one banana for a topping. To make the filling, place the rest of the bananas in the clean blender; add the coconut milk and blend on high until smooth. Then add the remaining filling ingredients, blending until the mixture is lovely and fine. Pour evenly into the tart pans and place in the freezer for 30 minutes until set.

For the caramel sauce, place the dates and water in the clean blender and whiz until combined. Add everything else and blend for 2–3 minutes, making sure the mixture is as smooth as possible and pourable. If it is not, add some more water.

Take the pies out of the freezer and pop them out of the pans. Slice the reserved banana half into rounds and place a few on top of each pie. Drizzle with the caramel sauce and sprinkle with some chopped nuts. Voilà!

159

# Sticky Toffee Apple Pie

We first made this for a friend's birthday party and they stopped just short of calling us liars when we told them what it was made from. It's one of those recipes that people just can't believe is natural – a sticky, indulgent, autumnal-flavored favorite.

For the crust

2 cups cashews

1 cup desiccated coconut

½ teaspoon Himalayan salt

¼ cup maple syrup

1 tablespoon maca powder

For the filling

2 apples, peeled, cored
  and diced

2 tablespoons coconut sugar

1 tablespoon lemon juice

½ teaspoon ground cinnamon

For the toffee sauce

1 cup pitted dates, soaked
  for 30 minutes or until
  very soft

3 tablespoons almond milk

2 tablespoons maple syrup

1 tablespoon maca powder
  (optional)

generous pinch of Himalayan
  salt

For the nut crumble

½ cup pecans

½ cup cashews

¼ cup almonds

For serving (optional)

dairy-free ice cream (see
  pages 112–113)

SERVES 8—12

Line an 8-inch pie dish with parchment paper.

Start with the crust. Place the cashews, desiccated coconut and salt in a high-powered food processor and blend on high until fine. Take out 3–4 tablespoons of this mixture and set aside in a bowl. Add the maple syrup, maca powder and a splash of water to the food processor and blend until well combined and the mixture sticks together. Press the crust mixture into the bottom and up the sides of the pie dish.

For the filling, place half the chopped apples and all the coconut sugar, lemon juice and cinnamon into the clean food processor and blend until broken up into small pieces. Transfer to a bowl and stir in the rest of the apple chunks.

Next make the toffee sauce. Place the dates in the clean food processor; add the remaining ingredients and blend on high for 3–5 minutes until very smooth. Pour into the bowl with the apple filling and stir together. Pour the apple-toffee mixture into the pie crust. Don't wash out your food processor – you'll need any toffee sauce left in it for the crumble.

For the nut crumble, pulse the nuts on high in the food processor until broken up into large chunks – the mixture will stick together slightly. Spread the crumble on top of the apple-toffee filling, then sprinkle the reserved crust mixture over the top. Place in the fridge for 1–2 hours to set. Serve chilled. Perfect with a scoop of one of our ice creams.

160

tarts, pies & pudding pots

raw cake

# Rhubarb & Raspberry Raw Crumble

Rhubarb is one of those vegetables (amazingly it is a vegetable and not a fruit) that we can't get enough of when it's in season. A Sunday without a crumble is a sad state of affairs and we're very proud of our take on this quintessentially English classic.

## For the filling
2 cups rhubarb chunks
4 tablespoons rice malt syrup or other liquid natural sweetener, plus more to taste
3 tablespoons coconut sugar
1 cup raspberries
½ cup pitted dates
½ teaspoon vanilla powder

## For the crust
½ cup pitted dates
1 cup walnuts
½ cup almonds
½ cup desiccated coconut
3 pinches of salt
1 tablespoon maca powder
½ teaspoon ground cinnamon
2 tablespoons rice malt syrup or other liquid natural sweetener

## For the crumble topping
½ cup walnuts
½ cup pecans
¼ cup pistachios
¼ cup coconut sugar
¼ cup hulled sunflower seeds
½ cup coconut flakes
½ tablespoon rice malt syrup or other liquid natural sweetener, if needed

SERVES 8–12

Preheat the oven to no higher than 110°F or to its nearest low temperature.

For the filling, mix the rhubarb, 2 tablespoons of the rice malt syrup and 2 tablespoons of the coconut sugar in a baking dish; place in the oven for 3 hours, until dehydrated and soft; then set aside. Meanwhile, toss the raspberries with the remaining 1 tablespoon coconut sugar and set aside.

For the crust, blend the dates and nuts in a high-powered food processor on high until fine. Add the remaining dry ingredients and blend again. Then blend in the rice malt syrup to help the mixture to stick together; if it's not sticky enough add a few drops of water. Press the mixture onto the bottom and sides of an 8-inch fluted tart pan. Place in the fridge for 2 hours to firm.

For the crumble topping, place all the ingredients except the coconut flakes and rice malt syrup in the clean food processor; whiz for a few seconds, just until the mixture is nice and chunky. Pour the crumble mixture into a bowl, add the coconut flakes and mix by hand until everything sticks together, adding the rice malt syrup if it doesn't. Set aside.

To finish the filling, blend the dates into a paste in the food processor; then blend in the rhubarb. Add half the raspberries, the remaining rice malt syrup and the vanilla and blend for a few seconds until just combined. Taste the mixture; add more syrup if desired. Gently stir in the rest of the raspberries. Pour the filling over the crust. Scatter the crumble on top. Press the crumble down gently and put the pie in the fridge for 1–2 hours to set.

163

# Mango, Lime & Avocado Mousse Tart

This is a light, zesty tart in which you can really taste the freshness of the fruit. The creamiest consistency is created by the avocado: You won't believe how good this is until you've tried it. Uniquely palate-cleansing, it's the perfect treat to end a light summer dinner.

### For the crust

1 cup macadamia nuts

1 cup pecans

¾ cup pitted dates, soaked for 30 minutes or until soft

¼ teaspoon vanilla powder

pinch of salt

### For the filling

3 small avocados, halved and pitted

1 large mango, peeled and pitted

½ cup coconut oil

½ cup rice malt syrup or coconut syrup

zest and juice of 1 lime

pinch of Himalayan salt

SERVES 8—12

Line an 8-inch pie dish with parchment paper.

First make the crust. Place the macadamia nuts and pecans in a high-powered food processor and blend on high until broken up. Add the dates, vanilla powder and salt and blend again until well combined and the mixture sticks together. Press the crust onto the bottom of the pie dish.

For the filling, scoop the flesh of the avocados into the clean food processor; blend until smooth. Add the remaining ingredients and blend until everything has been broken down and the mixture is silky smooth. Pour the filling mixture over the crust in the pie dish and place in the fridge for 2–3 hours until set.

164

# Orange Chia Marmalade Parfait

We first created this when experimenting with desserts for a summer garden party we were throwing. It was a hit, providing equal measures of refreshment and indulgence. Coconut cream and orange make for a deliciously light, fluffy texture – completed here with layers of marmalade and crumble.

### For the orange chia marmalade

1 seedless orange

1 tablespoon rice malt syrup or maple syrup

3 tablespoons chia seeds, plus more if needed

### For the orange cream

two 14-ounce (400 ml) cans coconut milk, refrigerated overnight; use the top layer of cream only

zest and 3 tablespoons juice from 1 orange

1 tablespoon rice malt syrup or maple syrup

### For the marinated oranges

1 orange, peeled and separated into segments

2 tablespoons orange juice

2 tablespoons coconut sugar

### For the crumble

¼ cup pecans

¼ cup almonds

¼ cup Brazil nuts

¼ cup coconut sugar

1 tablespoon maca powder (optional)

**MAKES 3 SMALL GLASS RAMEKINS OR JARS**

First make the chia marmalade. Grate the orange zest into a bowl. Peel the orange and add the segments to a high-powered food processor. Blend for just a few seconds to create a coarse pulp. Transfer to the bowl with the zest and stir in the syrup and chia seeds; mix well. Place in the fridge for 30–40 minutes or until the chia seeds have swelled and the mixture has a jam-like consistency. If it's still runny, add another tablespoon of chia seeds and place back in the fridge.

To make the orange cream, scoop the layer of cream on the top of the watery coconut milk into the clean food processor. Add the orange zest and juice and rice malt syrup and blend for just a few seconds until well combined and creamy – try not to overmix this. Transfer to a bowl and place in the fridge to firm.

For the marinated oranges, chop each orange segment into 3 chunks. Place in a bowl; stir in the juice and coconut sugar and mix together well. Set to one side until you are ready to assemble the parfait.

To make the crumble, place all the ingredients into the clean food processor and blend on high just until the nuts are coarsely chopped – keep this nice and chunky for some bite.

Assemble the parfait in small glasses or ramekins. Layer in the crumble, marinated oranges, orange cream, chia marmalade, orange cream and so on, sprinkling some crumble on top to finish.

165

# Avocado Cacao Ganache

The avocado ganache is a bit of a classic in the world of raw desserts. It's often the one that people choose to elicit that "OMG I can't believe it's not butter" reaction from first-timers. It has to be said that there's something pretty impressive about the transformation of the savory snack to sweet, silky cream at the push of a button.

## For the ganache

3 pitted Medjool dates

1 ½ medium avocados, halved and pitted

½ cup cacao powder

⅓ cup rice malt syrup or maple syrup

¼ cup coconut sugar

1 tablespoon maca powder (optional)

1 tablespoon chaga powder (optional)

½ teaspoon vanilla powder

2 pinches of salt

## For the cacao crumble topping

¼ cup pecans

¼ cup raw whole buckwheat groats

¼ cup goji berries

¼ cup pitted Medjool dates

2 tablespoons cacao powder

2 tablespoons coconut sugar

pinch of ground cinnamon

**FILLS 3 SMALL RAMEKINS**

To make the ganache, place the dates in a high-powered food processor and blend on high. Scoop the flesh from the avocados into the processor and blend to form a paste. Add all the remaining ingredients and keep blending until the mixture is nice and gooey. Transfer to a bowl and set aside.

For the crumble, add the pecans, buckwheat and goji berries to the clean food processor and blend on high until well combined. Add all the remaining ingredients and pulse until the mixture is nice and crumbly. It shouldn't be wet.

To assemble, spoon the ganache and crumble in alternating layers into 3 small ramekins, dividing equally and finishing with a layer of crumble. Place in the fridge until ready to serve.

166

# Passion Fruit & Pomegranate Parfait

Because of its sweet, appealing pastel hues, we like to serve this in individual glass jars at dinner parties. The pomegranate seeds are the *pièce de résistance* here, with their crunchy texture and juicy flavors. Choose jars with screw lids if you want to keep the parfait in the fridge for later. If left in the fridge overnight, it will become like a potted cheesecake – double win. *(Pictured on page 121.)*

For the pomegranate cream
½ cup cashews, soaked for
　1 hour, rinsed and drained
½ cup fresh pomegranate seeds,
　plus more for sprinkling
¼ cup coconut milk
2 tablespoons coconut syrup or
　rice malt syrup
¼ teaspoon vanilla powder

For the passion fruit cream
½ cup cashews, soaked for
　1 hour, rinsed and drained
¼ cup coconut milk
seeds from 2 passion fruit,
　plus more for sprinkling
2 tablespoons coconut syrup or
　rice malt syrup

**FILLS 3—4 SMALL JARS**

Make the pomegranate cream. Place all the ingredients in a high-powered blender and blend on high until completely smooth. Pour into small jars or glass ramekins, dividing equally. Sprinkle some pomegranate seeds over the top of each, and place in the fridge to set.

Make the passion fruit cream. Place all the ingredients in the clean blender and blend on high until smooth. Pour the mixture on top of the pomegranate layer in each jar.

Sprinkle some passion fruit seeds and pomegranate seeds over the passion fruit cream in each jar. Put in the fridge for 1–2 hours to set. Enjoy chilled.

167

# Coconut, Pistachio & Ginger Whip

Pistachio is one of our all-time favorite flavors. It's so delicate and when combined with ginger it has an extra sparkle. This is a light, whipped cream dream you won't be able to put down; these subtle flavors keep you coming back for more.

two 14-ounce (400 ml) cans
  full-fat coconut milk,
  refrigerated overnight; use
  the top layer of cream only
3 tablespoons rice malt syrup or
  maple syrup
¼ cup shelled pistachios
1 tablespoon ground ginger

**SERVES 2**

Scoop the layer of cream on the top of the watery coconut milk into a high-powered food processor. Whip until soft – don't overdo this. Transfer to a bowl.

Add the rice malt syrup and pistachios to the clean food processor and blend very briefly on high until the nuts are broken up and nicely incorporated, but still very chunky. Transfer this mixture to the bowl with the whipped coconut cream. Add the ginger and gently fold all together.

Spoon the whip into 2 small ramekins or jars to serve as a tasty ice cream alternative, or use the whip as a side to a pie or berry dessert.

169

# Crushed Berry Trifle

This is a raw dessert a British grandma would be proud of. Layers of rich flavors come together to form this towering superfood take on a classic trifle.

### For the chia berry mix

2 cups mixed fresh berries:
strawberries, blueberries,
blackberries, raspberries,
plus more for layering
2 tablespoons rice malt syrup or
other liquid natural sweetener
¼ cup chia seeds

### For the crumble

½ cup walnuts
½ cup pecans
¼ cup raw whole buckwheat
groats
¼ cup coconut sugar
2 tablespoons rice malt syrup or
other liquid natural sweetener
pinch of salt

### For the vanilla cream

½ cup macadamia nuts,
soaked for 1–2 hours, rinsed
and drained
½ cup cashews, soaked for
1–2 hours, rinsed and drained
½ cup filtered water
⅓ cup rice malt syrup or
other liquid natural sweetener
3 tablespoons coconut oil,
melted
2 tablespoons almond milk
1 teaspoon vanilla powder
1 teaspoon ground cinnamon

SERVES 3—4

To make the chia berry mix, place the berries in a high-powered food processor and blend on high for a few seconds only, so that they are still chunky. Add the rice malt syrup and whiz to combine. Transfer the mixture to a bowl and stir in the chia seeds, mixing well. Place in the fridge for 1 hour to set.

To make the crumble, place all the ingredients in the clean food processor and blend briefly, until coarse and still chunky. Set aside in a bowl.

To make the vanilla cream, place the macadamia nuts and cashews in a high-speed blender and blend on high until ground. Then add all the remaining ingredients and blend until the mixture is thick and creamy. Place the cream in the fridge for 2 hours until slightly firmer.

Assemble the trifle in either a large trifle bowl or 3–4 glasses or tall ramekins. First place a layer of crumble in each vessel, then some fresh berries, followed by some vanilla cream and then a layer of the chia berry mix; repeat until your glasses or the trifle bowl are full to the brim, finishing with a crumble layer and more fresh berries.

tarts, pies & pudding pots

raw cake

# Strawberry & Ginger Eton Mess

A traditional English dessert, Eton mess should be the eighth wonder of the world – a scrumptious melting pot of naughtiness. Creating this raw version was a big challenge: No matter how much we tried, we just couldn't get it as good as the original. A breakthrough came just as we were handing over the recipes for this book and we absolutely couldn't leave it out!

## For the meringue

liquid strained from one 14-ounce can chickpeas (reserve the chickpeas for another use)

3 tablespoons rice malt syrup

¼ cup lemon juice

¼ cup coconut sugar, ground in a blender until fine

## For the coconut cream

two 14-ounce (400 ml) cans coconut milk, refrigerated overnight; use the top layer of cream only

2 tablespoons rice malt syrup

½ tablespoon lemon zest, plus more for a garnish

1 teaspoon freshly grated ginger root

¾ cup quartered strawberries, plus more for serving

bachelor button petals, for a garnish

**SERVES 2**

Preheat the oven to no higher than 110°F or to its nearest low temperature. Line a baking sheet with parchment paper or aluminum foil.

For the meringue, pour the chickpea liquid, rice malt syrup and lemon juice into a large bowl and whisk with an electric mixer for 5–7 minutes, adding the coconut sugar 1 tablespoon at a time. Keep whisking until the mixture thickens and forms stiff peaks. Pour the mixture onto the baking sheet and place in the oven to dehydrate for 3–4 hours. Keep an eye on it as you don't want it to dry out too much or it will become sticky. When the mixture is dry to the touch and the edges can be cracked off, it is ready to take out and break into chunks.

To make the coconut cream, scoop the layer of cream on the top of the watery coconut milk into a high-powered food processor; add the rice malt syrup, lemon zest and ginger. Gently blend or pulse for a few seconds until the mixture becomes like whipped cream. Transfer the cream to a mixing bowl and gently fold in the strawberries.

To assemble, divide the coconut cream between two bowls or ramekins. Crumble in a few meringue pieces and fill to the top with more coconut cream, finishing off with more crumbled meringue and some quartered strawberries. You can assemble this dessert and leave in the fridge for 1–2 hours until ready to serve, or eat immediately. Decorate with bachelor button petals just before serving.

173

**tarts, pies & pudding pots**

# Strawberry Angel Whip

This is the non-powdered, natural sister of a packaged instant pudding that was a household favorite in 1970s' England. If you weren't lucky enough to have Angel Delight the first time round, this will more than show you what you missed.

5–6 large fresh strawberries

two 14-ounce (400 ml) cans coconut milk, refrigerated overnight; use the top layer of cream only

1 tablespoon coconut syrup

**SERVES 2**

Place the strawberries in a high-powered food processor and blend on high until they are coarsely chopped.

Scoop the layer of cream on the top of the watery coconut milk into the food processor, and add the coconut syrup. Blend until everything is smooth and combined.

Transfer the mixture to a freezerproof container and place in the freezer for 20–30 minutes until it has set slightly. Then spoon into two bowls or cups and serve straight away.

174

> *Coconut Cream*
> The thick layer of cream at the top of a can of coconut milk makes a great alternative to dairy cream in sweet dishes as well as savory, and it's just as indulgent, rich and velvety-smooth as its dairy equivalent.

tarts, pies & pudding pots

# Notes on Decorating & Styling

**We're always in awe** of how much difference the right decoration can make to the appearance of our raw creations. It really is the cherry on the cake, so to speak! We've had a lot of time to play around with our style and figure out what we think a cake by The Hardihood should look like. Of course, it's always changing based on the season or what we can get our hands on, but the idea is that the theme should run throughout. We like to think that if you had to pick a cake from a lineup, you'd know which one was ours.

**Using other recipes** as decoration
is a great way to enhance your cake.
Try brownie cubes or protein balls,
or save some of the base of a
cheesecake and roll it into mini balls
to use for toppers.

# Celebration Cakes

Our favorite thing about being in the business of cake making is that we're in the business of celebrations. We love being a part of someone's happiest moment. We hear from so many people that The Hardihood cakes have contributed to their birthday, wedding, engagement, hen party or baby shower being a huge success, and it really reminds us why we do what we do. Cake always gets an invite to the party, and preparing food for yourself or for others is an expression of love.

When decorating your raw cake the sky is the limit. We've become known for our minimalist style, but if you want to go all out and throw a decoration party, go for it. You've done the hard part in making the cake and you can let the fun part take center stage. Putting your own touch on your cake is a great expression of your creativity. For us, no two cakes are ever the same, and that's what keeps it exciting.

First, look at the cake that you've made, look at the colors and the flavors and think about what might complement it best. Perhaps it would look great to match the decoration to the flavor, using raspberries to decorate a berry-flavored dessert, or maybe some contrast is what it needs? Matching a bitter chocolate bark to a creamy sweet pie can offset the flavors wonderfully.

**Use cashew cream** (see page 80) to decorate your creation, applying it with a piping bag. Practise swirls, lines or zigzags etc., to find your favorite style. If you mess it up, you can simply scrape it off with the blunt side of a knife and try again.

## Ideas for cake toppers and sprinklers

— fresh edible flowers
— dried edible flowers, including bachelor button, rose or marigold petals
— desiccated or flaked coconut
— cacao nibs
— crushed nuts
— fresh herbs, as whole sprigs, picked leaves or chopped
— bee pollen (see note on safe use on page 181)
— any type of edible seed
— goji berries or other dried berries
— fresh berries or fruits
— dehydrated fruits
— piped cashew cream, flavored or plain
— cut-up pieces of raw cake or brownies
— chocolate sauce, drizzled on top
— chocolate bark

## Styling your photo for social media

If you want to share your creations with others, it's really worth going the whole hog and not just decorating your dishes but thinking about how you present them.

When styling a raw cake or treat for an Instagram snap, it's important to remember that everything in the photo will be noticed. Be sure to clear a space on your worktop or table – an uncluttered image will show off your creation much better. A white background or surface is usually our preferred setting, but a sheet of colored paper, a tea towel or a clean wooden table can look just as effective.

Lighting is key, so make sure you take your photo using as much natural light as possible – next to a window is ideal. If you're using your mobile, make use of filters or editing tools, experiment with them and find your favorite look. Your social media page will naturally start to look more cohesive if you use the same kind of editing techniques on every image.

**KEEP ME COLD**

179

**Edible flowers** are a game changer when it comes to decorating. They can make any dessert, breakfast or even a smoothie come alive. We love mixing them with herbs such as red amaranth for a luxurious, contemporary look.

notes on decorating & styling

# Glossary
of Ingredients

## Açai

Vibrant in color, this ancient purple berry grows on the palms of the açai tree, commonly found in the rainforests of the Amazon. We use it in powdered form for its deep luxurious hues and pungent berry flavor. Rich in antioxidants, it helps keep cells strong and aids them in fighting the invasion of free radicals. It is also high in vitamin C, vital for a healthy immune system.

## Adaptogens

Adaptogens are a unique group of herbal ingredients that support adrenal function and strengthen the body's response to stress. Working like a thermometer, they sense if things are heating up and so cool them down – and vice versa. Adaptogens need to be used regularly for a prolonged period of time before the effects can be noticed.

## Almonds

Rumor has it that almonds are the most popular nut in the world, and it's easy to see why. Sweet in flavor and either creamy when soaked or packing a satisfying crunch when lightly crushed, almonds are incredibly versatile. Although they were originally native to the Middle East, we tend to associate their milky flavor with European foods such as marzipan or amaretto. They're particularly high in vitamin E, which protects cell membranes and keeps skin and hair glowing. We always use them unblanched, with their skins.

## Apple Cider Vinegar

Apple cider vinegar comes from "apple must," which is basically the liquid strained from an apple that has been crushed with stem, skin and seeds intact. During the oxygenation and fermentation process the sugars in the apple turn first to alcohol and then to acetic acid, and this is what gives apple cider vinegar the health benefits it's known for. A great aid for digestion, it helps to kill pathogens, break up mucus in the body and clear the lymphatic system. Tangy and slightly moreish, it'll add a kick to any citrusy flavored tonic.

## Ashwagandha

Ashwagandha is an adaptogen from India and is, surprisingly, from the same family as the tomato. The root of the plant is dried and then powdered and used to tackle stress and anxiety and to promote relaxation and restoration. Add to an early evening brew to set you up for a good night's sleep or to a morning smoothie if you have a big day ahead.

## Astragalus

Astragalus is an adaptogenic herb that comes from a type of bean or legume. It protects the body from physical, mental and emotional stress and is the main ingredient of a popular Chinese medicine called Huang Qi. It's a powerful chi tonic and is used to fight colds, flu and other respiratory infections.

## Baobab

This African superfruit dries on the branch of the baobab tree, also known as the Tree of Life. The fruit is rich in soluble fiber that helps maintain digestive regularity and may function as a prebiotic. It's also rich in vitamin C, which supports skin health and collagen production.

We rely on it for its high level of antioxidants and love its tart, lemon-curd-like flavor.

## Bee Pollen

Bee pollen is the primary source of protein used to build a beehive. It is carried to the worker bees on the back of foraging bees where it is packed into pollen balls. Hugely nutritious, it contains nearly all of the nutrients required by humans, and is good for treating allergies, enhancing energy and soothing skin. It is worth noting that there's an ethical argument for not eating bee pollen as it was intended for growing the hive and one teaspoon of it takes one working bee eight hours a day for a month to gather.

*NOTE:* Bee pollen can provoke a severe reaction if you have a pollen allergy. Avoid if pregnant or breastfeeding, or if you are taking blood-thinning medication.

## Buckwheat Groats

Many people mistake buckwheat for a grain when it's actually an herb seed. Buckwheat is related to rhubarb and sorrel. It's naturally gluten- and wheat-free and full of trace minerals and vitamins. When eaten raw it adds a satisfying crunch to cake bases and dough as well as offering an inexpensive, nutritious way to add substance. If you'd like to sprout raw whole buckwheat groats, simply cover it in water for 30 minutes, rinse and drain, and then spread on a baking sheet and place in a 110°F oven for 2-3 hours to dehydrate.

## Brown Rice Syrup

Brown rice syrup comes from fermented brown rice in which the starch in the grains has been broken down. The liquid is removed and heated. Brown rice syrup is a natural sweetener but should be used sparingly.

## Cacao Butter

Extracted from the cacao bean, cacao butter is a pale yellow vegetable fat with a chocolatey taste. It's used to make chocolate and is solid at room temperature, which is helpful in raw recipes. It's calorific, but responsible for giving chocolate that melt-in-your-mouth sensation.

## Cacao Nibs

The cacao nib is what's left once the cacao bean that grows on the Theobroma cacao tree has been fermented, dried and roasted and the shells have been removed. Hugely nutritious and energy enhancing, the nibs boast large quantities of copper, magnesium, zinc and iron. We love them for their bitter but nutty flavor and use them to add texture and crunch to recipes.

## Cacao, Raw

Not to be confused with the more processed cacao, raw cacao comes from raw cacao pods that are sun-dried instead of roasted and then cold-pressed to separate the cacao from the cacao butter. It has a strong chocolate taste that smells divine but tastes bitter if unsweetened. It's a known heart-opener that may boost serotonin in the brain (this is known as the "feel-good" chemical, because of its positive effect on mood and emotion). Cacao has long been used as a health elixir and as a ceremonial medicine; the Olmeca people used it as far back as 1900 BC, before it became a ritualistic medicine used by the Aztec and Mayan cultures.

## Camu Camu

A small riverside-growing shrub found in the rainforests of the Amazon and Peru, camu camu is about the size of a lemon and is purple and orange in color. It's full of vitamin C, has antiviral properties, strengthens the immune system and balances mood. We use it powdered in smoothies and creams.

### Cashews

Native to the Amazon rainforest, India and the West Indies, cashew nuts grow from the bottom of the cashew apple. One of our favorite and most-used nuts, we go through an insane amount of cashews in our studio. They are hugely versatile: When soaked they become buttery and creamy with a delicate flavor, or when used dry their spongy texture adds a soothing, warming quality to a cake.

### Chaga

A powerful medicinal mushroom that grows on living birch trees, chaga takes 15–20 years to mature. It condenses many important nutrients and enzymes into a form that we can consume. High in antioxidants, this powerful adaptogenic improves immune response, is a great source of caffeine-free energy and promotes overall well-being.

### Chia Seeds

These nutritious little seeds come from the *Salvia hispanica* plant, which is related to mint. Borrowed from the Aztecs, they are known for their energy-giving abilities. Translated literally, chia means strength in Mayan. Easy to digest, they swell to a frog-spawn-like gel when soaked, creating a liquid that forms a nutritious base for puddings and potted desserts.

### Chlorella Powder

Native to Taiwan and Japan, chlorella is the antioxidant-rich compound that gives plants their green color. It improves circulation by increasing oxygen levels and encouraging cell rejuvenation. It also contains magnesium and

binds toxins and heavy metals, allowing them to be removed from the body.

### Cinnamon

There are two different kinds of cinnamon; we use more of the cassia cinnamon which is powdered from the branches or bark of several trees. The other comes in neat rolls and tends to be used more in traditional cooking. A flavorsome sweetener with warming, soothing qualities, cinnamon can be used to create a sense of homeyness and is great in festive or autumnal desserts. It has been used as a Chinese medicine treatment for colds and joint pain, and tests have given some support for its antibacterial and anti-inflammatory properties.

### Coconut Nectar

Coconut nectar is probably our favorite sweetener because it needs no lengthy heat treatment to concentrate its flavor. It comes from the flower of the coconut palm and is dark in color and extremely sweet, with not even a glimmer of coconut flavor.

### Coconut Oil

Virgin, cold-pressed coconut oil is a staple in raw dessert making, as it's an extremely nutritious fat that can be found in the flesh of the coconut. It contains antimicrobial lipids that have antifungal, antibacterial and antiviral properties. It's primarily made up of medium-chain triglycerides that are easier for your body to digest and turn into energy. It's a rich alternative to butter or cream with a smooth texture. Coconut oil is solid at room temperature and turns to liquid if it is even a degree or two warmer (see page 15 to melt it). It is a staple in raw dessert making because of its versatility.

## Coconut Sugar

Coconut sugar doesn't come from the actual coconut, but instead from the flower of the coconut palm. It begins life as coconut nectar before being dehydrated to form a mineral-rich powder. The texture of coconut sugar is quite coarse, but a few seconds in a high-powered blender will turn it into a fine dust reminiscent of powdered sugar, which is great for fluffy creams and raw chocolate. Coconut sugar smells divine and has a rich, caramel flavor, which adds a lot to a dessert. It's low on the glycemic index and far more nutritious than any other powdered sugar, for sure.

## Cold-Brew Coffee

Making cold-brew coffee is deceptively simple – it is made just by replacing heat with time. In this raw process, coffee beans are cold-water brewed for 18–24 hours. While the flavor compounds and some caffeine from the beans are extracted, the bitter oils and fatty acids are left behind, making the brew smoother, more alkaline and easily bottled and transported. If you haven't time to do this, you can use strong coffee brewed the usual way instead.

## Cordyceps

Cordyceps is a healthy fungus with a fascinating backstory, known for improving drive, endurance and confidence. Traditionally it could only be formed when a caterpillar became infected with cordyceps spores, which would consume the entire caterpillar until all that was left was a caterpillar-shaped mushroom. Today scientists know how to cultivate cordyceps in a laboratory.

## Dates

Another crucial component to raw baking, dates are sticky, sweet and hugely versatile. Grown on the date palm, they dry on the branch before being gathered by hand and sorted for quality. They're rich in many vital nutrients and are one of the sweetest fruits. We use dates as a binding agent in a lot of our desserts. (If they are hard, we soak dates until soft: 10 minutes in warm water, up to an hour in cold water.) Make sure the dates you're choosing haven't been preserved with sulphites and be sure to remove the pits; this is particularly easy to do once they've been soaked. Drain soaked dates before adding to your recipe. Rich in flavor, dates taste like a luxurious caramel.

## Desiccated Coconut

Brilliantly white and boasting all the health benefits of coconut, desiccated coconut is the finely grated, unsweetened fresh meat of the coconut that has been dried. It's inexpensive and its almost pearlescent glow is perfect for frostings, decoration and adding texture to protein balls or cake bases.

## Echinacea

Most people know echinacea for its cold-fighting reputation, but it can also be used as a daily immunity booster and a painkiller. Made from a mix of active substances, several species of the plant are used to make supplements from the flowers, leaves and roots. We add it to morning tonics to support and uplift throughout the day.

## Filtered Water

When you're going to the effort of making sure that the ingredients you use are close to nature, it makes sense to apply the same logic to the water you drink. Although we're hugely lucky to be in the 90 percent of the world's population who have access to clean water, it's worth noting that the tap water we drink contains potentially harmful contaminants, pesticides and hormones. The ideal solution is to have a filtration system installed in your house, but failing that a readily available Brita filter is the second-best option.

## Flax seeds

Golden flax seeds (also known as linseeds) come from the flax plant, which grows in cooler climates, and although they can be found split or as an oil we prefer to work with the powdered version for optimum absorption. Powerhouses of nutrition, flax seeds are one of the richest known plant sources of omega-3 fats, which are essential for brain development and promote heart and joint health. They're also known as nature's answer to hormone replacement therapy and can be used to balance estrogen levels, particularly for women going through menopause.

184

## Ginger

Fresh ginger root is a seriously flavorsome ingredient and surprisingly fruitful when juiced. It is the underground rhizome of the ginger plant. It has a firm, fibrous texture and a little goes a long way. It's known for its anti-inflammatory, immunity-enhancing qualities and is great for settling an upset stomach. We also find it helps clear the sinuses in the winter months. Use it to add spice and zing to juices, protein balls and recipes in which you'd rather not use too much added sweetener.

## Ginseng

There are 11 different varieties of ginseng, all of which are characterized by their slow-growing, fleshy roots. Some places sell the ginseng root whole, and although this is a great way to check the quality it's much easier for your body to digest the powdered version. Ginseng is said to improve brain function, thinking and cognition. Traditional medical practitioners also recommend it for lowering stress levels and improving physical and mental energy.

## Goji Berries

Goji berries can be bought as a juice or as a dried fruit, they're beautifully bright in color and have a sweet but mellow flavor. Native to the Himalayan mountains of Tibet, they're said to be anti-inflammatory, antibacterial and antifungal. They've been used in Chinese medicine for 6,000 years, but are now readily available in most supermarkets. When soaked they swell to almost double their size. We use them decoratively or in pudding pots.

## Hazelnuts

Hazelnuts are one of the most expensive nuts out there and for that reason they're a bit of a special-occasion nut for us. Synonymous with autumnal flavors and Nutella, the pale kernels are packed full of healthy oils, vitamin E and minerals. With a luxuriously rich, chocolatey flavor, they can be used to raise the quality of any dish, sweet or savory.

## Hemp Seeds

Typically found in the Northern Hemisphere, hemp comes from a variety of the cannabis plant that is not to be confused with its naughty sibling. Hemp seeds are packed with minerals that help to rebuild and repair cells in the body. A fantastic source of protein, hemp seeds can also be bought in powder form, which is a great addition to raw desserts. With a mild, nutty flavor and as a great source of essential fatty acids, we use hemp powder if we feel we need grounding.

### Himalayan Salt

Harbouring 84 of the same trace minerals and elements in the same proportions that can be found in the human body, Himalayan salt is known to stimulate circulation, lower blood pressure and remove heavy metals from the blood. We add a pinch to pretty much everything; it adds depth and contrast and always makes desserts tastier.

### Lemon

Steadfast staples in our morning routines, lemons are rich in vitamin C and rejuvenate and uplift from within. A great blood purifier, antiseptic and alkalizer, lemons cleanse the digestive tract as they draw out toxins and support the immune system.

### Lucuma

Lucuma powder comes from the Peruvian lucuma fruit, which looks like a cross between a mango and an avocado in its whole form. A source of antioxidants, minerals and fiber as well as healthy carbohydrates, we love using the powdered form for its maple-flavored sweetness. In fact, In Peru lucuma is actually the most popular flavor of ice cream because it is so delicious.

### Maca

Maca is one of our favorite superfood powders; it smells incredible and has a subtle sweetness and malty fudge-like flavor. Native to the Andes, it is part of the broccoli and watercress family and actually looks like a robust radish in its natural state. The Incas and Peruvians called it the food of gods because of its energy-giving abilities. It's said to be great for migraines, fertility and sex drive. You can sprinkle maca on top of pretty much anything to make it taste creamier.

### Macadamia Nuts

Macadamia nuts are native to Queensland, Australia, where they grow near streams. With similar qualities to cashews, these nuts are a great substitute for those who are cashew sensitive; they're both soft and absorbent, with a mild, delicate flavor.

### Maple Syrup

Maple syrup comes from the sugar maple tree, which is prevalent in Canada and the States. A hole is drilled into the tree in early springtime (sugaring season), when the days are warm but the nights are cool, and the sugar-circulating fluid – or sap – drips out, is harvested, taken to a sugar house and then boiled until the water evaporates, leaving behind the rich, sweet syrup, which is then filtered. It takes 40 gallons of sap to make 1 gallon of syrup.

### Matcha

This bright green powder comes from Japanese tea leaves that are grown in the shade to increase chlorophyll content and are then hand-picked before being dried and ground. We've found matcha to be a bit of a Marmite character when it comes to flavor: some love it, others hate it. However, we're big fans and even though we know it's expensive we can't help but use it unsparingly. It is rich in antioxidants and has a concentrated caffeine kick.

### Pearl Powder

Literally powder made from crushed pearls, use of pearl powder dates back to ancient Chinese skincare and medicine. A powerful antioxidant, it contains signal proteins that stimulate the regeneration of collagen. As you'd expect, it's pretty pricey, but it is one of those super-special purchases if you stumble across it.

## Pecans

The pecan tree is native to Mexico and southcentral and southeastern areas of the US and is from the same family as the walnut. Pecans are characteristically sweet in flavor and smooth in texture.

## Pistachios

Another luxurious nut, pistachio is popular not only for its succulent, sweet flavor, but also for its desirable color palette. We love its washed-out, pastel hues as much as we love its soft mouth feel. A member of the cashew family, we purchase shelled pistachios for easy access.

## Probiotic Powder

This is a powdered dose of natural, live, good bacteria that helps promote gut health and prevent some associated ailments. When digestive flora is in check, we feel happier and lighter and energy that would otherwise be spent supporting digestion is free to assist with the other functions of the body, such as detoxification and healing. Make sure you use a good-quality probiotic. Some poorer-quality products may contain dead rather than live bacteria. Look for brands that are stored in the fridge and are high in live, active cultures.

## Pumpkin Seeds

Most people are quite familiar with pumpkin seeds, but perhaps not so familiar with their range of benefits. With a chewy texture and mellow flavor, pumpkin seeds are a valuable source of magnesium and omega-3, which promotes restful sleep.

## Reishi

Reishi is another medicinal mushroom and is one of the most powerful adaptogens out there.

It gets the immune system to work more effectively rather than blindly stimulating it. Some champion it for its meditative qualities, promoting calmness and balance within the body.

## Schisandra

Native to northeast China and parts of Russia, the schisandra berry grows on a climbing vine. Used widely in beauty products because of its reputation for skin-protecting qualities, it's also thought to be particularly beneficial to kidney, lung and liver function. It has a sweet and tangy taste and complements strawberry flavors well.

## Spirulina

Rumor has it that spirulina is one of the oldest life forms on Earth. It's basically an edible powdered algae that grows in saltwater lakes in Africa and Mexico; it uses light, warmth, water and minerals to produce protein, carbohydrates, vitamins and other vital nutrients. Spirulina is reputed to be good for a whole host of serious conditions, including heart disease, cancer, high cholesterol, high blood pressure, anemia and raised blood sugar levels. We love it for its deep velvety green color and smooth, savory flavor. In some smoothies we find it tastes like candy, but maybe we've just been doing this for too long.

## Sprouted Chickpeas

Chickpeas can be used raw and sprouted, or if time is short, from a can. To sprout chickpeas, soak the dried peas in filtered cold water and leave overnight, then drain and rinse thoroughly. Spread out on a baking tray, cover with a tea towel, and leave for at least 12 hours to sprout. They're a brilliant source of protein and magnesium and have a fulfilling texture when ground.

### Sprouted Oats

The difference between sprouted oats and ordinary breakfast oats is in the production process. Normally whole oats are steamed before being rolled, but sprouted oats are simply soaked to unlock the nutrients, slowly dried and then rolled to retain more flavor and nutritional value. Ordinary rolled oats can be used if you don't have the sprouted variety.

### Tahini

Tahini paste is made from sesame seeds that have been ground to a butter, thus releasing their oils and flavors. It's high in vitamins and minerals and lighter on the palate than nut butters. We use it to add a savory touch.

### Tulsi

Tulsi, also called holy basil, is such an all-round performer that it's been labeled the Queen of Herbs; it's known to sharpen memory and promote the removal of mucus from the bronchial tube. It can be used to treat the common cold, flu, sore throats and chesty coughs as well as balance moods. The leaves and the seeds of the plant are equally valuable. We prefer It In Its powdered form, added to smoothies, teas and desserts. It is sweet in flavor and reminiscent of mint liquorice and Earl Grey tea.

### Turmeric

We love turmeric – a knobbly root vegetable famous for its bright yellow color and incredible anti-inflammatory qualities. We use it juiced or powdered at the onset of a sniffle and we also find it alleviates joint pain. Its citrusy, spicy flavors work well with lemon and ginger and it makes the best natural food coloring. Be careful though: Turmeric stains anything and everything it touches.

### Vanilla

The vanilla pod grows alongside fragrant flowers on a tropical climbing orchid. Once picked it is often ground down to a powder and sold as the second most expensive spice in the world after saffron. This heartwarming, luxurious flavor doesn't get enough credit in our opinion; there's nothing plain about the beautiful, homely notes of vanilla. We use it in everything, from our cheesecakes and mousses to chocolate-flavored treats, and we prefer the powder to the more processed liquid extract, and sometimes use the seeds right from the pod.

### Walnuts

After almonds, walnuts are said to be the second most popular nut in the world. They grow inside fruits on trees of the genus *Juglans* and are thought to be particularly good for brain health, giving fuel to the argument that food resembles the organs it benefits. This is partly because walnuts contain a unique concoction of powerful antioxidants. Check the quality of walnuts before buying them, and steer clear of those that look shriveled. They're one of the more perishable nuts and can quickly lose their luster.

### Wheatgrass

Wheatgrass comes from the young shoot of the wheat plant. Full of chlorophyll, vitamins and nutrients that help protect the cells from oxidative stress, it's reputed to have a positive effect on digestion, the formation of red blood cells and restoring pH balance. Its mild, pale, lime green color can be used as a natural food coloring as its flavor isn't overpowering.

# Index

188

192

## ACKNOWLEDGMENTS

THANKS TO:

Dom Chung for the "in"

Danielle, Marina, Ellen and Lydia for helping with the leftovers

Ingrid for the man-hours

Jeremy for the storytelling and (mostly) good advice

Cathryn for imagining this book before we could

Mads for the guinea pig duty

Charlotte, Lizzie, Jemima and Amber for the art

Jones & Sons for being the savory to our sweet

And the rest of our friends and family who've put up with us
talking about nothing but cake since 2014 — we couldn't have done
this without your unwavering support and enthusiasm.

The universe, for always having our backs.